The Idea of Socialism

To my sons Johannes and Robert, who have made
everything easier from the very beginning

Axel Honneth
The Idea of Socialism
Towards a Renewal

Translated by Joseph Ganahl

polity

First published in German as *Die Idee des Sozialismus. Versuch einer Aktualisierung* © Suhrkamp Verlag, Berlin, 2015

This English edition © Polity Press, 2017

Polity Press
65 Bridge Street
Cambridge CB2 1UR, UK

Polity Press
350 Main Street
Malden, MA 02148, USA

ISBN-13: 978-1-5095-1212-6

The Idea of Socialism
Library of Congress Cataloging in Publication Control Number: 2016044974

A catalogue record for this book is available from the British Library.

Typeset in 11 on 14 pt Sabon by
Servis Filmsetting Ltd, Stockport, Cheshire
Printed and bound in the UK by CPI Group (UK) Ltd, Croydon, CR0 4YY

The publisher has used its best endeavors to ensure that the URLs for external websites referred to in this book are correct and active at the time of going to press. However, the publisher has no responsibility for the websites and can make no guarantee that a site will remain live or that the content is or will remain appropriate.

Every effort has been made to trace all copyright holders, but if any have been inadvertently overlooked the publisher will be pleased to include any necessary credits in any subsequent reprint or edition.

For further information on Polity, visit our website:
politybooks.com

Contents

v

"COURAGE yet, my brother and sister!
Keep on – Liberty is to be subserv'd whatever occurs;
That is nothing that is quell'd by one or two failures, or
    by any number of failures,
Or by the indifference or ingratitude of the people, or by
    any Unfaithfulness,
Or the show of the tushes of power, soldiers, cannon,
    penal statutes.

What we believe in waits latent forever through all the
    continents,
Invites no one, promises nothing, sits in calmness
    and light, is positive and composed, knows no
    discouragement,
Waiting patiently, waiting its time."

> Walt Whitman, "To a Foil'd European
> Revolutionaire" [1856], *Leaves of Grass*

Preface

As recently as a century ago, socialism was such a powerful movement that there was hardly any great social theorist who did not see the need to address it in detail – sometimes critically, sometimes sympathetically, but always with great respect. John Stuart Mill was the first to do so in the nineteenth century, followed by Emile Durkheim, Max Weber, and Joseph Schumpeter, to name only the most important. Despite significant differences in their personal convictions and theoretical orientations, these thinkers agreed that the intellectual challenge socialism represented would have to permanently accompany capitalism. Today things look much different. If socialism finds any mention at all in social theory, it is taken for granted that it has outlived its day. It is considered unthinkable that socialism could ever again move the masses or be a viable alternative to contemporary capitalism. Virtually overnight – Max Weber would not believe his eyes – the two great nineteenth-century rivals have switched roles: Religion is perceived as the ethical force of the future, whereas socialism is regarded as a creature of the past. My belief that this is an overly hasty reversal and thus cannot be the whole truth is one of the two motives of this book. I will attempt to show that socialism still contains a vital spark, if only we can manage to extract its core idea from the intellectual context of early industrialism and place it in a new socio-theoretical framework.

My second motive for writing this book is the reception of my most recent, comprehensive study *Freedom's Right*.[1] Over the course of the numerous discussions about the book, I have been told that my methodological point of departure in the normative horizon of modernity betrays just how little my critique aims to transform the current social order.[2] Whenever necessary and possible, I have already responded to these objections in print, arguing that they are based on a misunderstanding of the methodological restrictions I have consciously imposed upon myself.[3] Yet I still felt the need to demonstrate that we only need to slightly adjust the perspective of *Freedom's Right* in order to open it up to an entirely different social order. Contrary to my original intention, therefore, I saw the need to follow up my larger study with a smaller one, which would more clearly define the vision entailed by the lines of progress already reconstructed from a strictly internal perspective.

For these two reasons I accepted an invitation to give the Leibniz lectures in Hanover in 2014, which I used as an opportunity to renew the basic ideas of socialism. I am very grateful to my colleagues at the Institute of Philosophy in Hanover, especially Paul Hoynigen-Huene, for allowing me to use their yearly lecture series to deal with what was most certainly an unfamiliar topic for them. I profited greatly from the discussions following the three lectures and gained a clear sense of the changes and additions I would need to make in order to present a second version of my lectures which would offer a much richer set of perspectives on a revised socialism. A cordial invitation by Rüdiger Schmidt-Grépály to accept the Distinguished Fellowship of the Friedrich Nietzsche Kolleg in Weimar in June 2015 gave me the opportunity to present the revised version of my text to a larger audience. A parallel seminar with students from the "Studienstiftung des deutschen Volkes" at the Wielandgut Ossmannstedt near Weimar enabled me to engage in several extremely fruitful discussions and to gather a number of suggestions for final corrections. I am very thankful to the participants in this seminar as well as to the director and the staff at the Kolleg for the interest they showed in my work.

I owe my gratitude to all the friends and colleagues for their advice during the production of the manuscript. Above all I would like to thank Fred Neuhouser, a close friend and trusted colleague in the Department of Philosophy at Columbia University, who gave me strong encouragement and a number of helpful suggestions from the very beginning of my work on the text. I have also profited greatly from the critical comments on the first version of my lectures made by Eva Gilmer, Philipp Hölzing, Christine Pries-Honneth and Titus Stahl. I am very grateful to them all for their years of help and attentiveness. Hannah Bayer and Frauke Köhler supported me as always by gathering literature and aiding in the production of the manuscript. To them I am grateful as well. Finally, for this English edition I would like to especially thank Joseph Ganahl, who has worked with perfect timing and again done a wonderful job translating the book; additionally I am grateful to Kristina Lepold who came up with good solutions for translating some difficult German formulations into English.

Axel Honneth, June 2015

Introduction

Our contemporary societies are characterized by a puzzling divide. On the one hand, discontent with the current socio-economic state of affairs, with contemporary economic and working conditions, has increased enormously in recent years. More than ever in the post-war era, people are outraged at the social and political consequences unleashed by the global liberalization of the capitalist market economy. On the other hand, this widespread outrage seems to lack any sense of direction, any historical sense of its ultimate aim. As a result this widespread discontent has remained oddly mute and introverted, giving the impression that it simply lacks the capacity to think beyond the present and imagine a society beyond capitalism. The disconnect between this outrage and any notion about the future, between protest and a vision of a better world, is a novel phenomenon in the history of modern societies. Ever since the French Revolution, major social movements have been motivated by utopian visions of a future society. Here we might think of the Luddites, Robert Owen's cooperatives, council communism and other communist ideals of a classless society. But today, these currents of utopian thinking, as Ernst Bloch would have put it, seem to have been interrupted. Although the outraged have a clear sense of what they do not want and what outrages them about current social conditions, they have no halfway clear conception of the goal to which the change they desire should ultimately lead.

Finding an explanation for such a sudden decline in utopian energy is more difficult than might appear at first sight. This can hardly be due to the collapse of communist regimes in 1989, to which intellectual observers like to refer when they proclaim the end of all hopes for a society beyond capitalism. Those who are outraged at the growing divide between private wealth and public poverty, though without having a concrete idea of a better society, certainly do not need the fall of the Berlin Wall to be convinced that the social welfare provided by Soviet state socialism came at the cost of a lack of freedom. Moreover, the fact that a real alternative to capitalism did not exist until the Russian Revolution did not prevent people in the nineteenth century from dreaming of peaceful coexistence in justice and solidarity. So why should the bankruptcy of the communist bloc have caused this apparently deep-seated capacity for utopian transcendence to wither? Another oft cited cause for this peculiar lack of vision is the abrupt shift of our collective sense of time. According to this claim, our entry into "postmodernism" – starting in the world of art and architecture and spreading into the broader culture – has devalued characteristically modern conceptions of teleological progress and paved the way to a consciousness of eternal recurrence. This new, postmodern conception of history supposedly hinders visions of a better life, since we have lost the notion that the inherent potential of the present necessarily strives to expand beyond itself and point the way towards an open future of continuous progress. Instead, the future is seen as having nothing to offer but reprises of past life-forms and social models. However, the very fact that we have become accustomed to advances in medicine or the enforcement of human rights casts doubts on this presumption. Why should transcendental imagination be alive and well in these fields, and yet impossible when it comes to the question of whether society can be reformed? The claim that we now have a fundamentally altered sense of history assumes that we can no longer anticipate a new and different kind of society, thus ignoring the strong, though certainly exaggerated hopes in the global implementation of human rights.[1] A third explanation could thus refer to the difference between these two fields, i.e. between a structurally neutral establishment of internally sanctioned rights and a reorganization of basic social institutions, in order to draw the conclusion that it is only in the latter sphere that utopian forces have slackened. My impression is that this comes closest to the truth, though without capturing it completely, for we still need to explain why the current socio-political material should be unsuitable to utopian expectations.

It might help to recall that current economic and social events appear far too complex and thus opaque to public consciousness to be capable of intentional transformation. This is particularly true when it comes to processes of economic globalization in which transactions are carried out too quickly to be understood; here a kind of second-order pathology seems to make institutional conditions appear as mere givens, as being "reified" and thus immune to any efforts to change them.[2] On this view, Marx's famous analysis of fetishism in the first volume of *Capital* is only applicable today, as the general sense that social relations essentially consist in "the form of a social relation between things"[3] did not exist as long as the workers' movement still regarded society as capable of change – as is demonstrated in their dreams and visions.[4] Reification, therefore, only applies to the present state of capitalism. If this were true, as everyday observations and empirical analyses indeed seem to suggest,[5] we are unable to anticipate social improvements in the basic structure of contemporary societies because we regard the substance of this structure as being impervious to change, just like things. On this account, the inability to translate widespread outrage at the scandalous distribution of wealth and power into attainable goals is due neither to the disappearance of an actually existing alternative to capitalism, nor to a fundamental shift in our understanding of history, but rather to the predominance of a fetishistic conception of social relations.

This third explanation, however, still does not explain why traditional utopian conceptions no longer have the power to dissolve or at least make a breach in reified everyday consciousness. For more than a century, socialist and communist utopias electrified their addressees with visions of a better form of life, making them immune to feelings of resignation. The extent of what people view as "inevitable" and thus necessary about their social order depends largely on cultural factors, particularly on political patterns of interpretation which show that what appears inevitable is in fact any-

thing but. In his historical study *Injustice*, Barrington
Moore gives a convincing account of how German
workers' sense of hopelessness began to disappear once
powerful re-interpretations of contemporary conditions
demonstrated that institutional givens were in fact subject to arrangements and negotiations.[6] This makes the
question as to why classic and influential ideals have lost
their power to unmask and destroy the phenomenon
of reification all the more urgent. To pose the question
more concretely, why do visions of socialism no longer
have the power to convince the outraged that collective
efforts can in fact improve what appears "inevitable"?
This brings me to the main topic of the following four
chapters of this brief study. Two related issues appear
to me to be of particular intellectual relevance today:
first, the internal or external reasons for the seemingly
irrevocable loss of the power of socialist ideas to inspire;
second, the conceptual changes needed to restore the
vitality these ideas have lost. To do so, however, I will
need to reconstruct the original idea of socialism as
clearly as possible (section I). Only then can I turn to
the reasons why these ideas have become so antiquated
(section II). In the two concluding chapters I put these
antiquated ideas back on their feet by making a number
of conceptual renovations (sections III and IV). It should
also be noted that the following considerations have a
metapolitical character, since I make no attempt to draw
connections to current political constellations and possibilities for action. I will not be dealing with the strategic
question of how socialism could influence current political events, but solely how the original intention of
socialism could be reformulated so as to make it once
again a source of political-ethical orientations.

I

The Original Idea: The Consummation of the Revolution in Social Freedom

The idea of socialism is an intellectual product of capitalist industrialization. It first saw the light of day after it had become apparent that the demands for freedom, equality and fraternity raised in the course of the French Revolution remained unfulfilled promises for large parts of the population. But in fact, the term "socialism" was introduced much earlier to philosophical discourse when, in the second half of the eighteenth century, Catholic theologians sought to expose the German theory of "natural law" as a dangerous misconception. At this time, the polemical expression "socialistae" (a neologism derived from the Latin "socialis") referred to a tendency in the works of Grotius and Pufendorf, who were accused of claiming that the legal order of society should be founded on the human need for "sociality" rather than divine revelation.[1] A direct line runs from this critical use of the term to the legal textbooks of the late eighteenth century, in which the term "socialist" is primarily used to refer to Pufendorf and his pupils. Yet by this time the term had already lost its polemical connotation and merely come to indicate the intention of giving natural law a secular foundation in the human need for sociality.[2] Thirty years later, in the 1820s and 1830s, when the English terms "socialist" and "socialism" entered the European vocabulary, any relation to their original use in debates on natural law had been lost.[3] Robert Owen in England and the Fourierists in France referred to themselves as socialists as if they had invented a new term, expressing no intention of engaging in philosophical debate over the justification of law. "Socialist" and "socialism" thus became "terms for a movement directed towards the future" (Wolfgang Schieder), an expression of the political aim to make the existing society more "social" by establishing collective organizations.

Of course, efforts to make society more "social" had been undertaken long before the first half of the nineteenth century. Here we might think of the Scottish moral philosophers who sought to derive the principles of a well-ordered society from sentiments of mutual sympathy. Even the young Gottfried Wilhelm Leibniz, who in no way can be suspected of being a socialist, flirted with such notions when he wrote up plans to establish intellectual clubs he termed "Sozietäten". Following the Platonic model of the rule of philosophers, these organizations – later deemed "academies" – were meant to serve the common good not only by performing certain educational and cultural functions, but also by embedding the economy in a social framework.[4] In the brief manuscript "Society and Economy", written in 1671, Leibniz assigned to these academies the task of providing financial support and a minimum wage to the poor, thus putting an end to the competitive

economic struggle and ensuring "true love and trustful-
ness" among the members of society.[5] Certain passages
of Leibniz's text give the impression that he virtually
anticipated the radical aims pursued by Charles Fourier
150 years later, who intended to establish cooperatives
called "phalanstères".[6]

In making plans for a cooperative society, however,
Fourier was faced with an entirely different set of prevailing social values from Leibniz's feudal surroundings.
After all, the French Revolution with its principles of
freedom, equality and fraternity had given birth to
moral demands for a just social order that could be
invoked by anybody seeking to improve social conditions. Thinkers and activists in 1830s France and
England who began to refer to themselves as "socialists" were fully aware of their debt to the values
established by the revolution. Unlike Leibniz or other
social reformers prior to the French Revolution, whose
designs conflicted directly with the political reality of
their day, these socialists could invoke already institutionalized and universally confirmed principles in order
then to derive radical consequences from them. From
the very beginning, however, it was unclear just how the
demands of these "early socialist" groups related to
the three norms established by the French Revolution.
Although the intellectual exchange between the followers of Robert Owen in England, the Saint-Simonists and
the Fourierists in France went back as far as the 1830s,[7]
their respective conceptions of desirable social change
were too distinct to count as a shared goal.

For all three of these groups, their rejection of the
post-revolutionary social order derived from their outrage at how the expansion of the capitalist market

prevented a large portion of the population from taking advantage of the principles of freedom and equality proclaimed by the French Revolution.[8] "Degrading", "shameful" or simply "immoral" were the terms they used to describe the fact that workers and their families – both in the countryside and in the towns, and despite their willingness to work hard – were left completely vulnerable to the arbitrariness of landowners and private factory owners concerned solely with profit, thus imposing upon the majority a life of constant need and the ever-present threat of further impoverishment. Emile Durkheim offers what is perhaps the best initial formulation of the common denominator shared by all of the above-mentioned currents of early socialism: In a number of well-known lectures, this French sociologist attempted to define the essence of "socialism" underlying the various socialist doctrines, proposing that they all shared the aim to subordinate economic functions, which had managed to escape all social control, to the authority of society as represented by the state. According to Durkheim, as distinct as the various socialist currents might have been, they all agreed that the only way to put an end to the misery of the working masses was to reorganize the economic sphere, thus subjecting economic activities to the greater social will.[9] Even if this definition of socialism does not yet adequately capture its normative intention, it does reveal the common ground shared by all "socialist" movements and schools of thought. Whether we consider Robert Owen and his followers, Saint-Simonists or Fourierists, all of these groups traced the injustice done to the working population back to the fact that the capitalist market had managed to slip out of the control of the broader society, instead obeying solely the laws of supply and demand.

Yet, if we take a closer look at the shared vocabulary of the various currents of early socialism, then it becomes immediately apparent that Durkheim does not even attempt to explain their links to the ideals of the French Revolution.[10] Throughout the text he treats these groups as if they were solely concerned with the largely technical issue of how to socially re-embed the market, as if they did not also aim to realize the principles of liberty, equality and fraternity for the entire population – historically the more obvious aim. Similar attempts to grasp the chief ambitions of socialism also fail to understand the true moral motives of its proponents. John Stuart Mill and Joseph Schumpeter are typical in this regard, both displaying a conspicuous tendency to reduce the socialist project to the desire for a more just distribution of resources, without going into any more detail about the underlying moral or ethical intentions of this project.[11] And yet the early thinkers who called themselves "socialists" were driven by genuine normative principles they felt they could derive from the demands of the French Revolution, a fact that becomes immediately clear once we take a closer look at how they argue for their positions. Robert Owen, more of a practitioner than a theorist, and certainly the least influenced by the French Revolution, justified his labor cooperatives in New Lanark by claiming that the experience of working for each other would teach "mutual benevolence" to the lower classes and thus solidarity even with strangers.[12] Similar to Owen, though with a much stronger socio-philosophical grounding, Saint-Simon and his followers were convinced that workers' lack of freedom under capitalism could only be overcome in a social order in which a centralized plan would ensure that all be paid according to their abilities, thus bringing about a "universal association" of mutually responsible persons.[13] Finally, Fourier and his students justified their plans for a cooperative society by arguing that only free associations of producers, the previously mentioned "Phalanstères", could satisfy the demand that all members of society cooperate freely.[14] Nowhere in these justifications for socialist aims is the collectivization of the means of production an end in itself. To the extent that this measure is taken into consideration at all, it is only as a necessary precondition for entirely different, moral demands. This primarily concerns the first and the last principles of the French Revolution, "liberty" and "fraternity", whereas "equality" often plays a subordinate role. One even gets the impression that the three socialist groups were already content with the fragmentary legal equality of their day and instead strove to erect on this foundation a community of solidarity between producers who recognize each other's abilities and contributions. The background to these moral conceptions is a belief that only plays a marginal role in early socialist writings, but which nevertheless represents an important source of their agreement. The early socialists all assumed that the largely legal notion of individual freedom was far too narrow for it to be reconcilable with the principle of fraternity. With a bit of hermeneutic goodwill, we could say that the three early socialist groups discovered an internal contradiction in the principles of the French Revolution due to its merely legal or individualist understanding of freedom. Though they might not have been very aware of it, these socialists all sought to expand the liberal concept of freedom in order to reconcile it somehow with the aim of "fraternity".

Their aim to reconcile the principles of "liberty" and "fraternity" by reinterpreting the former becomes even more apparent in the second wave of socialism. Both Louis Blanc and Pierre-Joseph Proudhon, who otherwise followed very different paths,[15] justified their critique of the expanding market economy by arguing that its characteristic understanding of freedom is reduced entirely to the pursuit of purely private interest, to "l'egoïsme individuel", as Blanc puts it.[16] Both were convinced this prevented any meaningful change to the grim economic conditions of the time. Moreover, they felt that under these circumstances the officially existing claim to "fraternal" coexistence could not be fulfilled. Therefore, Blanc and Proudhon felt that the task of socialism was to resolve a contradiction in the demands of the French Revolution: The aim of fraternity, of mutual responsibility in solidarity, cannot even begin to be realized as long as liberty is understood solely in terms of the private egotism characteristic of competition in the capitalist market. Blanc and Proudhon's plans to either supplement or replace the market with other forms of production and distribution[17] were therefore intended primarily as a way to realize a kind of "freedom" in economic relations that no longer conflicted with the demand for "fraternity". The contradiction in the moral demands of the French Revolution could only be removed if individual freedom was no longer understood as the private pursuit of interests, but rather as a relation in which the pursuits of individual members of society complement each other in the economic power-center of the new society.

The Original Idea

If we take a look back at Durkheim's definition of the basic idea of socialism, we see that although the French sociologist was right to claim that all socialist projects share the intention of bringing economic activities back under the control of the larger society, he overlooks the normative reasons underlying this intention. Early socialists demanded that the economic sphere be subjected to social directives not only in order to fend off the evils of a merely partial moralization of society, one that stops short of the threshold of the economy, nor merely to ensure a more just distribution of resources by means of a new economic order, but rather to ensure that production serve the moral purpose of stripping the liberty proclaimed by the French Revolution of its merely private and self-interested character. Instead, freedom was to be understood as a form of free cooperation, thus reconciling it with the other revolutionary promise of fraternity.[18] Viewed from this perspective, the socialist movement has always been based on an immanent critique of the modern, capitalist social order; it accepts the latter's normative bases of justification – liberty, equality and fraternity – but argues that these values cannot be fully reconciled with each other as long as liberty is not interpreted in a less individualistic and more intersubjective manner.

The works of these authors, however, offer little basis for an understanding of this new concept of freedom, the crucial element of the entire socialist movement. These early groups employed categories such as "association", "cooperation", and "community" in order to make clear that their very different economic models were based on the principle that the self-fulfillment of each must depend on the self-fulfillment of the other. However, they made no conceptual effort to elucidate the forms of intersubjective interlinking that would overcome the liberal, individualistic understanding of freedom. Proudhon goes one step further, stating in *Les confessions d'un révolutionnaire* (1849) that "liberty and solidarity are identical expressions from a social perspective".[19] Proudhon adds to this obvious reference to the French Revolution by stating that, contrary to the declaration of civil rights in 1793, socialists understand the "freedom of each" not as a "limitation", but as an "aid" for the freedom of all others.[20] Proudhon, however, immediately loses sight of this conceptual proposal once he goes on to call for the founding of people's banks that enable such intersubjective freedom by granting interest-free loans to small workers' cooperatives. Here he seems to define the individual freedom of the other as a kind of support, but not as a condition for the fulfillment of my own individual freedom.[21] Proudhon wavers between two different alternatives to the individualistic concept of freedom depending on whether a free act can be regarded as already having been completed prior to being supplemented by others, or whether it needs the supplementation of others to count as a completed act. The structure of the given "association" or "community" that would enable a society to become "social" by reconciling liberty and fraternity will turn out to be different depending on which of these versions we choose. In the first case, the community consists of free members whose cooperation gives them additional inspiration and support, but not freedom. In the second case, cooperation in the community is the social condition allowing the members of society to become completely free by mutually supplementing each other's still incomplete actions.

Neither the early socialists nor Proudhon take adequate account of such differentiations in their accounts of "social freedom", as I would like to call it from now on. They are entirely aware that the project of the bourgeois revolution can only be fulfilled by overcoming the individualism of capitalistic freedom and making it reconcilable with the demand for fraternity. However, they lack the conceptual means to offer a concrete account of what it would mean to predicate the achievement of individual freedom on coexistence in solidarity. The young Karl Marx was the first to take this step when he, at about the same time as Proudhon, set out to clarify the theoretical foundations of the new socialist movement.[22] For this Parisian exile, who was very familiar with the attempts of his French peers to justify the socialist project, his German origins did not represent a challenge when it came to explaining the aims of their shared project. Marx largely refrained from employing terms such as "fraternity", "liberty", or "solidarity", drawing instead on contemporary attempts in his home country to carry on the Hegelian tradition. His familiarity with the idealism naturalistically reinterpreted by Feuerbach gives his account greater conceptual clarity, but also makes its political-moral thrust more opaque. Nevertheless, Marx makes perfectly clear even in his early works that the concept of freedom employed in traditional economics and implemented in the capitalist market represents a kind of individualism irreconcilable with the demands of a "true" community encompassing all members of society. Therefore, the writings of this young exile in the 1840s can be understood as a further step along the path to developing the idea of socialism immanently, i.e. on the basis of the contradictory aims of the liberal social order.

In one of his most important texts from the 1840s, a text that has recently received much attention, Marx comments on James Mill's book on political economy and explains what he himself has to criticize about the current state of society and how he instead envisions an intact society.[23] Here Hegel's influence on Marx is even more explicit than in his famous "Paris Manuscripts", which is reflected by the use of two different modes of mutual recognition to characterize the two contrasting social models. In capitalist society, individuals relate to each other only indirectly by exchanging their products on an anonymous market with the aid of money. To the extent that they pay attention to other market participants at all, they see only the abstract qualities of the others' business acumen and self-interest, not their concrete needs and individuality. Marx states that in this society, making an ironic allusion to Adam Smith, each member is only a "merchant" for the other.[24] Here the recognition that members owe each other as members of an integrated community merely consists in the mutual affirmation of their respective right to "plunder" each other. The members of this society do not supplement each other in their "social relationship" through their respective individual acts; rather, they perform these acts merely "with the intention of plundering", as Marx puts it bluntly.[25]

In this first part of his considerations, Marx merely repeats the arguments his socialist predecessors used to analyze how the market economy prevents "fraternal" social relationships or "solidarity" in Hegelian terms. Because market participants encounter each other as subjects interested solely in their own private advantage, they are incapable of feeling sympathy for each other and offering each other the support required by social relationships of fraternity or solidarity. In order to express this suppression of solidarity even more drastically, Marx employs a notion from the *Phenomenology of Spirit* and claims that "our mutual recognition" takes on the form of a "struggle" in which "the victor is the one who has more energy, force, insight, or adroitness".[26]

Towards the end of his ingenious commentary, Marx begins to outline relations of production in which the members of society recognize each other's individual needs rather than their private egotism. The anthropological background to this account consists in an idea that Marx adopts from Feuerbach and perhaps from Rousseau, which holds that the satisfaction of human needs almost always requires the complementary action of other subjects. Once the social division of labor has attained a certain degree, I can only satisfy my hunger if others produce food for me; my desire for adequate housing can only be fulfilled by the cooperation of several different craftsmen. Marx claims that this mutual dependence is systematically concealed by capitalist relations of production: Although subjects produce in order to satisfy economic demand, and thus the needs underlying this demand, they are not motivated by concern for the needs of others, but solely by their own egocentric interest in increasing their own utility. According to Marx, matters would be very different if goods were not exchanged on the market and through the medium of money. In this case each producing subject would be directly faced with the needs of others, such that each member would directly experience his particularly human dependence on others both in his own actions as well as in the anticipated reaction of the others.[27] Although Marx only states that members of society would have "affirmed" themselves "in two ways", he obviously has in mind relations of production in which humans mutually recognize each other's individual needs. In an "association of free producers", as he puts it in his later writings, the members of society would no longer relate to each other merely through the anonymous intertwining of their respective private aims, but through their shared concern for the self-realization of all others.[28]

By accentuating Marx's line of thought in this way, we can pick out those general elements in his concrete, rather vague economic model that indicate a concept of social freedom. Like his socialist predecessors, Marx viewed freedom merely as the least restricted way of realizing one's own aims and intentions; he also agrees with his comrades that in capitalism, freedom means viewing others as mere means, thus violating the already institutionalized principle of fraternity. In order to resolve this internal contradiction, Marx envisions a social model in which freedom and solidarity are interlinked, in which each individual can view his own aims as the condition for the realization of the aims of others. This means that individual intentions must be so clearly interlinked that we can only achieve our aims cooperatively, conscious of our dependence on each other. However, as the reference to "love" at a central point in the text[29] also makes clear, this relation of solidarity encompasses not only the implementation but also the formulation of our aims. Just as in love, my activities must both serve my own self-realization as well as that of my partners in interaction; otherwise, the freedom of the other would not be an object of conscious concern for me.

This critical point in Marx's model can be made even more explicit if we draw on the comparison Daniel Brudney makes between Rawls and Marx. In Brudney's view, social communities can be differentiated according to whether the members relate to each other by means of either overlapping or intertwined aims.[30] In the first case, subjects pursue shared goals they can achieve in unity, though without intentionally pursuing those goals in a unified manner; according to the classical view, the market represents a good example of this kind of collective goal-realization. Here the mechanism of the "invisible hand" is supposed to ensure that the participants can pursue their own economic interests while simultaneously serving a higher purpose, i.e. the general welfare. By contrast, intertwined aims demand that the members of society make these aims the maxim or purpose of their own individual actions. In this case, as Brudney claims, the subjects not only act with each other, but "for each other"; they act directly and consciously to achieve commonly shared purposes. In the first case, that of overlapping aims, the fact that my actions contribute to the realization of our shared aims is a contingent effect of the pursuit of my own intentions; in the second case, that of intertwined aims, the same result arises as a necessary consequence of my conscious intentions.

It is this latter model of social communities upon which I believe Marx bases his alternative to the capitalist social order. To formulate these differences in the language of the mutual recognition he continually uses in his commentary on James Mill's political economy:

Whereas in the market economy individuals realize shared aims by merely recognizing each other as individual utility-seekers, thus systematically denying their mutual dependence, in an association of free producers the members would realize their shared aims by intentionally producing for each other on the basis of their mutual recognition of each other's needs, thus performing their own individual actions for the sake of those needs. Even if Marx himself does not state it explicitly, to me it seems obvious that he believed his alternative model enabled the fulfillment of a goal that, despite the best efforts of his socialist predecessors, remained out of their reach. Marx believed he had managed to expand and reformulate the concept of individual freedom, the existing social order's principle of legitimacy, so as to ensure that it ultimately and necessarily coincides with the requirements of coexistence in solidarity. At this point, we must systematically examine whether this model of social community can truly fulfill the claim to have reconciled individual freedom and solidarity in a new way.

For the time being, however, we will leave aside the fact that the early representatives of socialism all sought to anchor the principle of social freedom in the sphere of societal labor. As if the reproduction of society as a whole could be organized in this sphere alone, they ascribed no independent role to political democracy, and thus saw no need to examine more carefully whether other forms of freedom had already been institutionalized in the political sphere. But before I go into this congenital defect of the socialist project, I will first deal with whether the model of social freedom outlined above represents a viable alternative to the individualism of liberal conceptions of freedom. Did first-generation socialists truly develop an independent, novel understanding of freedom? Or did they merely improve upon what is normally indicated by the term "solidarity" or, to use the more antiquated term, "fraternity"? The premise of the liberal model of freedom consists in an idea which at first sight seems undeniably true: We can only speak of individual freedom in a meaningful way if subjects are free to pursue their aims without any hindrance. This freedom is limited, in the first place, only by the condition that the consequences of our actions must not impinge on the freedom of other subjects. Therefore, liberalism places the general guarantee of individual freedom in the context of a legal order ensuring that individuals can act without interference as long as they do not interfere with the equal claim of others to enjoy this same freedom. This original liberal model becomes more complicated once Rousseau and, following him, Kant come along, both of whom believe we cannot speak of individual freedom as long as actors' decisions derive from natural instincts rather than their own intentions. Both thinkers thus impose on freedom the additional condition that subjects' decisions to act themselves must represent acts of self-determination which ensure that their aims are determined entirely by their own reasoning.[31] All early socialists apparently agreed with this transition from a "negative" to a "positive" understanding of freedom, as Isaiah Berlin later termed the step taken by Rousseau and Kant, thereby warning against taking it.[32] Even if these socialists did not know each argument in favor of the new model, they were aware of Rousseau's "contrat social" or Kant's moral philosophy; they regarded it as self-evident that individual freedom requires that our aims be open to reason and not dictated by nature. When it comes to the definition of what is "rational", however, they do not follow Kant's proposals. They do not agree that individuals must morally examine their own maxims in order for their actions to be "free". Instead they seem to follow Rousseau – or Hegel, in Marx's case – who assumes for different reasons that individuals' intentions are free if they are aimed at satisfying either uncorrupted or "natural" needs, or if they correspond to the given historical stage of reason.[33] For the socialists, therefore, individual freedom in the first instance merely indicates the ability to realize one's own free, more or less universally shared intentions through actions that need only respect the rights of others to the same kind of freedom.

The special twist that Proudhon and Marx in particular give to this model of positive freedom derives from a much more comprehensive idea about the nature of the unjustified constraint which prevents subjects from realizing their free intentions. According to the conception of early liberalism, this constraint primarily consists of social barriers such as a personal or institutional authority that imposes its own will on other subjects.[34] In the republican tradition upheld today by authors such as Quentin Skinner or Philip Pettit, the extent of what can count as coercion is expanded to include even the influencing of the wills of others; "freedom as non-domination" is the formulation that now customarily characterizes the republican understanding of freedom.[35] Socialists go far beyond this approach and assume that coercion can even include situations in which a person's rational intentions, which therefore demand realization, are hindered by the opposing intentions of others. On this account the individual realization of rational aims within the society as a whole can only be considered free if it is agreed to by all others and can only be fully realized by means of their aid and support. Individual freedom therefore only exists if it, in Hegel's words, becomes "objective", i.e. if the other members of society can no longer be viewed as potential limitations to one's own intentions, but rather only as partners whose cooperation is required to realize these intentions.[36]

It is at this point that socialists bring to bear their own particular concept of community, a concept that they always mention in the same breath as freedom. However much their respective terminology might differ, they always understand "community" to mean more than what is generally characterized by the term – not just as a set of shared values and a certain degree of identification with the aims of the group, but primarily as a feeling of mutual responsibility and sympathy. And we have already seen the fundamental socialist notion that the aims of the members of a community not only overlap, but are intersubjectively intertwined, such that they do not merely act "together" [*miteinander*], but "for each other" [*füreinander*].[37] Which connection, therefore, do the socialists draw between this model of community and their concept of freedom?

One possibility is to conceive of a community of solidarity as a necessary condition for the exercise of the above-mentioned freedom. Joseph Raz presents a weaker form of this thesis in his book *The Morality of Freedom*, leaving out the elements of mutual sympathy in his concept of community. There he argues that individuals cannot make use of their autonomy as long as they do not live in a social community which offers concrete possibilities for realizing their aims.[38] But socialists want more. They not only regard cooperation in the community as a necessary condition for freedom, but also as the sole way of exercising true freedom; in their mind, nothing else even deserves to be called freedom. Social freedom therefore means taking part in the social life of a community whose members are so sympathetic to each other that they support the realization of each other's justified needs for each other's sake. This makes freedom an element in an holistic individualism. On this account, freedom – the free realization of one's own intentions or aims – cannot be realized by individuals at all, but only by a collective of the kind just described, without this collective having to be regarded as an entity that is superior to its individual elements.[39] Although the social group as a whole becomes the medium of the freedom they think of as a property, capacity or achievement, the existence of this group derives solely from the interaction of individual subjects. However, the collective only becomes a bearer of individual freedom if the community manages to instill certain modes of behavior in its members, thus institutionalizing that behavior. First and foremost, this includes mutual sympathy, such that each person is concerned about the self-realization of the others for non-instrumental reasons. According to the socialists, the establishment of these forms of interaction in the social community will remove all the negative aspects of capitalist society. If subjects practice mutual sympathy, they will necessarily treat each other as equals and thus refrain from exploiting or instrumentalizing each other in any way.

The original idea of socialism is rooted in the notion

that in the future it will be possible to organize entire societies on the model of communities of solidarity. This idea boldly unifies the three partially conflicting demands of the French Revolution in a single principle by interpreting individual freedom as a kind of freedom in which each person complements the other, completely resolving this freedom with the demands of equality and fraternity. The point of departure of the socialist movement is the holistic notion that the community of solidarity, rather than the individual, is the bearer of freedom. All the measures, in good times and bad, that would later seek to eliminate the evils of capitalism were intended to create a society whose members supplement each other and treat each other as equals. Because of this link to the demands of the French Revolution, bourgeois critics have always had difficulties simply discounting the aims of the socialist movement. After all, these critics appealed to the same normative principles in their own efforts to establish a democratic constitutional state. Even today, accusations that socialists worship collectivism or entertain an idyll of community remain somewhat insipid, as they seem to intentionally deny the fact that the principles of legitimacy which prevail in contemporary society include not only freedom, but also – admittedly vague – conceptions of solidarity and equality.[40]

On the other hand, early socialists made it easy for their critics by failing to give a sufficiently persuasive account of their original, groundbreaking idea. The accounts they presented in the first half of the nineteenth century were too flawed to prevent the rapid emergence of objections that could not be ignored. As we have already seen, not only did early socialists restrict the community of solidarity entirely to the economy, ignoring the question of whether a more complex society could in fact be organized and reproduced entirely from within the economic sphere. For reasons that are hard to understand, early socialists simply ignored the entire sphere of political deliberation, thus never sufficiently clarifying the relationship between the economic sphere and hard-fought political freedoms. Furthermore, the founding fathers of the socialist project – primarily Saint-Simon and Marx – burdened this project with a metaphysical theory of history which made it more or less impossible to understand their own intellectual contributions as experiments in introducing change in capitalist societies. Because they were convinced that the revolution was inevitable in the near future, they saw no cognitive or political benefit in attempts at gradual change in the present. Among these deficits in the original socialist program, we can distinguish those that derive entirely from the early industrial context in which they emerged from those that are much more profound and relate to the structure of the idea itself. In the following chapter, I will discuss three birth defects of the socialist project in order to then judge which of them can be eliminated by adapting them to our time, and which require more thorough-going conceptual revisions. My aim is to get an overview of the corrections that could once again restore some of socialism's former vitality.

II

An Antiquated Intellectual Structure: The Spirit and Culture of Industrialism

As I have attempted to show in chapter I, the normative intuitions of the early socialists went far beyond traditional conceptions of distributive justice. Instead they sought to either reform or overcome the capitalist market economy by means of revolution, creating social relations which would realize the aims of the French Revolution. This was to be accomplished by creating a relationship between liberty, equality, and fraternity in which these principles would mutually enable each other. The motto for reconciling these three principles, brought into conflict with each other by the prevailing economic order, is "social freedom". According to this principle, human beings cannot realize their individual freedom in the matters most important to them on their own. The satisfaction of generally shared needs depends on intersubjective relationships that are only "free" under certain normative conditions – the most important of which is the mutual sympathy found only in communities of solidarity. Otherwise, individual subjects could not rely on the free and willing satisfaction of their needs by the complementary actions of others. The members of society must not only act "with each other", but also "for each other", for this is the only way they can satisfy their shared needs freely. Socialism, therefore, has always been based on the notion of a communitarian life-form, rather than merely a more just system of distribution.[1] Before I turn to the theoretical framework surrounding the normative intentions of early socialists, I want to discuss this intention itself in more detail so as to defend it against a number of probable objections.

At the end of the first chapter, I characterized the notion of making individual freedom dependent on other subjects, of turning freedom into "social" freedom, as a theoretical element of holistic individualism. Picking up on the work of Philip Pettit, this term indicates a socio-ontological position which claims that the realization of certain human capacities requires the existence of social communities and thus holistic entities, but without drawing the conclusion that individual subjects as such are incomplete or even non-existent.[2] This concept of social freedom differs from collectivism in that it is primarily concerned with the conditions for the realization of individual freedom. It also differs from traditional individualism in that it regards this freedom as being contingent on participation in a certain type of social community. Characteristic of the intermediate position developed by early socialists, the term freedom plays a decisive role on both levels at the same time, that of the individual and of the social community. Individual subjects can only realize their capacity for freedom as members of a free social community, i.e. a community in which the reciprocal fulfillment of generally shared intentions is without compulsion and thus takes place in an atmosphere of mutual sympathy.

Contrary to what might be presumed, this conception of freedom does not depend on small communities in which all the individual members know each other personally. Although it might appear as if such mutual sympathy would require a degree of intimacy afforded only by personal acquaintances, the very fact that we speak of nations or political movements as communities demonstrates that this initial suspicion is unjustified. Intimate trust is hardly necessary in order to think of oneself as a member of a community of solidarity in which each person is concerned about the needs of the others. As Benedict Anderson has shown, it is enough for the members to regard each other as sharing certain common aims, regardless of how large the given collective is and whether the members of that collective are in fact personally familiar with each other.[3] It is obvious that people can be concerned about the well-being of other community members not only in small, family-like groups, but also in large, anonymous communities; we need only recall that redistributive measures in favor of those who are worse off always require feelings of "solidarity" or "fraternity". For instance, John Rawls states at a number of places in his *Theory of Justice* that the application of his Difference Principle presupposes relationships of "fraternity" among the citizens.[4]

The idea of social freedom that the socialist movement brought onto the political stage thus does not depend on the problematic assumption of small communities. It can easily be applied to entire societies, though we must clarify its relationship to other possible forms of freedom and to social reproduction in general. This is the point at which socialism's faults and conceptual shortcomings arise – the issue I will be dealing with in the present chapter. I will largely be referring to the tradition of Western Marxism, in which the birth defects of the socialist project had already become apparent to sympathetic critics by the 1920s.[5] In order to get at the problematic legacy of socialism, however, we must go one step back and briefly clarify the social and historical framework within which socialists developed this new and revolutionary concept of social freedom. All protagonists of the socialist movement, from Robert Owen and Proudhon to Karl Marx, agreed that the key to creating social relationships of solidarity lies in the reform or the revolutionary overcoming of the capitalist market economy. These economic institutions were held to be solely responsible for the egotistical narrowness of the prevailing understanding of freedom. Therefore, the establishment of a cooperative life-form that fulfills revolutionary promises can only begin here. Furthermore, socialists agreed that the motives and the willingness to overcome capitalism could already be found in the prevailing social relations; they assumed that workers, producers and managers desired to replace the capitalist market with some kind of cooperative economic system. This second assumption turns the socialist doctrine into a mere expression or reflection of an oppositional force already present in society, which means that the relationship between theory and practice would consist in educating, informing or enlightening a clearly defined social group. Finally, all proponents of the socialist movement share the assumption that the changes they seek to make are historically necessary to a certain degree: The capitalist market will either be destroyed by the crisis it creates, unleash economic forces of collectivization, or produce ever stronger resistance as a result of impoverishment. Whatever their explanations for the impending self-destruction of capitalism, hardly any of the intellectual pioneers of socialism refrained from assuming the historical necessity of their vision in the near future.

If we combine these three background assumptions, we get a rough idea of the understanding of society and history underlying early socialists' conception of social freedom. Focusing almost exclusively on the economic sphere, they assumed that capitalism alone was responsible for the fact that the newly gained freedom was understood merely as the freedom to pursue one's own private interests. Yet within this economic sphere, socialists discovered a proletarian movement that sought to collectivize the economy and resist the way in which capitalist competition had undermined social bonds. The socialist doctrine could thus attach itself as a kind of reflexive organ to the workers' movement in order to foster – by means of strategic enlightenment and education – a historical process thought to lead necessarily to the cooperative transformation of the relations of production, which would eventually lead to a community based on the principle of mutual benefit. Certainly not every proponent of socialism would have agreed to all of these fundamental socio-theoretical assumptions. Despite a great deal of agreement about the normative principle of social freedom, there was much debate about whether the process of economic collectivization already underway should be viewed as a process of gradual reform or as the first steps toward a revolution, and what kind of economic relations were entailed by

an association of all producers. Particularly with regard
to this last point, socialist conceptions varied widely
depending on what they saw as the economic cause of
capitalism's susceptibility to crises, and thus also on how
they proposed to organize economic reproduction on a
socialized basis.[6] But the three assumptions mentioned
above still form the cornerstones of the socio-theoretical
horizon within which early socialists developed their
common idea of social freedom: the economic sphere
as the locus of the struggle over the appropriate form of
freedom; the reflexive attachment to an already present
oppositional movement; and, finally, the historical-philosophical expectation of the inevitable victory of the
movement. I will now take a look at each of these three
premises in greater detail in order to examine the consequences for an alternative social model. Here my first
aim will be to scope out the socio-theoretical burden
early socialists handed down to the workers' movement
by virtue of developing their original idea of social freedom in a framework defined by these three assumptions.

1. As we have seen, early socialists including Karl
Marx tended to interpret the right to liberty established
by the French Revolution exclusively in terms of the
legal permission to pursue one's own interests within
the economic sphere on the basis of private property.
This capitalist system, which in their view had become
the true refuge for the new individual freedoms, is then
contrasted with the vision of a cooperative mode of
production in which subjects no longer act against each
other, but for each other, thus realizing what I have
termed social freedom. Because these thinkers address
both the supposedly merely private and egotistic freedoms and the new, social freedoms exclusively with

reference to the economy, their accounts raise a problem that will soon prove to be more serious than might appear at first sight. They rob the entirely different sphere of democratic popular rule, which Rousseau and his revolutionary successors had reserved for the new right of individual self-determination, of any normative value, setting it aside as a negligible element of social reproduction. Because these socialists one-sidedly locate both the good and the bad forms of freedom solely in the economic sphere, they deprive themselves unintentionally of the chance to think of this new regime, in which shared goals are negotiated democratically, in categories of freedom. The inevitable result is not only an inadequate understanding of politics, but also a failure to grasp the emancipatory potential of these same rights to freedom. The consequences of this assumption are so important to the later fate of socialism that they require a more detailed elucidation.

Already in the work of Saint-Simon and his followers, the Saint-Simonists, socialist theory seems to shift the focus entirely from the political sphere to that of industrial production. Accordingly, technical advances in industry and trade are viewed as necessitating the abolition of the last remainders of feudal rule and its economic inefficiencies, replacing them with a new social order in which both industrial workers and managers could work together according to a plan to satisfy the needs of even the worst off. The premises for such a transformed, cooperative mode of production were to be brought about by a central bank in which a representative body, recruited from industry, would make any political steering [*Steuerung*] superfluous. After all, the well-being of the nation would be brought about by the allocation of credit.[7] Just like Saint-Simon and his followers, who furnished their technocratic theory with the aura of a new civic religion, subsequent generations of socialists were hardly interested in the political function of the newly acquired civil rights. Like the Saint-Simonists, who represented a virtual religious sect, they felt the reorganization of society according to the principle of solidarity would have to take place entirely within the economic sphere, where private egotism would be replaced by mutual supplementation in the satisfying of needs, thus denying political institutions their steering function. Here as well, Proudhon, who had already found the clearest way of expressing this new concept of freedom before Marx, went the furthest by demanding the immediate abolition of all government activities that could be replaced by mutual cooperation between small producing communities. As a consequence, he no longer saw any need for the political rights declared by the revolution; in his eyes they merely served the interests of private property owners on the capitalist market and would lose their role with the establishment of the cooperative mode of production.[8]

While Fourier, Louis Blanc and Auguste Blanqui also show a certain disdain for the newly gained political liberties, it is Marx who elevates the problem to an entirely new level of discussion. In his essay "On the Jewish Question", published in 1844 and representing a milestone in the socialist movement, Marx investigates the significance of the Jews' struggle for political equality for future socialist aims.[9] Marx's answer has two different levels, the first of which addresses this problem in terms of given social relations, the second of which with regard to emancipated society. Making reference to the present and employing Hegel's vocabulary in the *Philosophy of Right*, Marx claims that "civil society", i.e. the capitalist market economy, and the "state" exist in two separate spheres, each of which is subject to a different set of principles. Marx believes that as long as these institutional tasks remain distinct, the efforts of the Jewish minority to integrate into society are clearly important for the goal of emancipation, since the achievement of equal rights obviously represents a great step forward.[10] However, he also believes that these efforts at integration will lose any positive function once the isolated tasks of the state have been brought back within the sphere of a true human community. Under these conditions, the unfortunate division of individuals into "citoyens" and "bourgeois", into citizens of the state and private economic subjects, will have been abolished. Furthermore, an association of all cooperating members of society will be able to take care of any political and administrative tasks, obviating the need for a higher authority which would grant them the right to self-determination. This last step in Marx's argumentation is particularly important for our purposes: Liberal rights to freedom, which according to Marx "proclaim that every member of the people is an equal participant in popular sovereignty",[11] lose all normative value in socialist society, because there would no longer be a separate sphere of common will-formation apart from the economy, which would in turn mean that individuals would no longer require a right to self-determination.[12]

Because of this degradation of the liberal rights to freedom that Marx himself long regarded as worthy of struggle, as well as the institutional division between the political and the economic sphere, the socialist movement inherited a heavy burden that it could no longer so easily shake off. Because the hope for reconciling freedom and solidarity rested entirely on the prospect of a communitarian reorganization of the economic sphere, socialists felt they could dissolve all individual rights into a cooperative community, leaving no legitimate place for the autonomy of the individual, nor for the intersubjective exploration of a common will. Regardless of which founding socialist document we examine, we always find the same tendency to deny any role for liberal rights to freedom, and thus for will-formation among free and equal citizens. In this new form of the social, subjects are integrated into society solely by means of their participation in the cooperative process of production. Although they can realize their social freedom in this sphere, they can no longer be concerned with their individual self-determination. The consequence of this social vision was the incapacity to find any access to the values of the political sphere. It would take several decades for the movement to begin to fill this gap by adding the adjective "democratic" to the "socialism" for which they fought. But even the term "democratic socialism", which German Social Democrats did not make official until after World War II,[13] only provided a stopgap solution to the problem they had inherited from the party's founders. They still could not present a conception of social freedom capable of motivating a critique of capitalistic private egotism without completely denying the value of individual rights to freedom. Instead, this double concept of democratic socialism usually claimed that traditional liberal democracy should be understood as the sphere in which a parliamentary majority needed to be won in order to then resolve the "social question" by imposing restrictions on the capitalist market. This put an end to the much more radical demand that the economy be a sphere of cooperation rather than competition.[14] An altogether different approach at this crucial point would have been to abandon the views of socialism's founding fathers and further develop the idea of socialism by drawing on Hegel's theory of freedom. This would have allowed socialists to interpret liberal rights to freedom not as a restriction but as a necessary condition of economic social freedoms.[15] Perhaps there would have even been a chance to subject not only the economic sphere, but also the process of democratic will-formation to the principle of social freedom.[16] But before I turn to this alternative left untouched by the socialist tradition (chapter IV), I want to address the second premise of the social theory of early socialists.

2. Saint-Simon and his adherents also offer the first indications of the second premise of early socialist social theory, according to which these thinkers' own ideals in fact represent the actual interests of an oppositional movement already present in contemporary society. The Saint-Simonists were convinced that the entire class of industrial workers – from the unskilled laborers to the managers – were just waiting for the moment when their common activities and abilities would finally be freed from the yoke of a feudal-bourgeois property order in order to increase their productivity in free association. Against the background of this presupposed process of emancipation, Saint-Simon's doctrine provides the additional knowledge and the almost religious certainty required to finally bring about the collectively desired community of all producers.[17] This same presupposition

also shows up in the works of Robert Owen, Louis Blanc and Pierre-Joseph Proudhon. The only difference is that they restrict the revolutionary community to industrial workers. Just like in the works of Saint-Simon and his adherents, these socialists believed that industrial workers shared a common interest, even before the socialist idea of pushing social development toward the free cooperation of all producers could take effect.[18]

Certainly, socialist theory in itself has no problem establishing links to resistance movements which represent the theorists' own ideals. In fact, part of the reflexive structure of any theory so clearly directed toward the future is that it searches within social reality for the desire to make its own claims come true in actuality, thus bringing about the state of society anticipated by the theorist. Yet early socialist authors did not content themselves with exploring reality for such resistance movements, but rather they apodictically presupposed them. These theorists claimed that even before their theory takes effect in practice, the interests and desires they sought to justify and bring to fruition already existed objectively in social reality. The only way to speak of these pre-scientific attitudes in an objective manner, however, is to merely ascribe them. But then we are no longer dealing with empirical interests, nor with actual desires, but with intentions that social groups are assumed to pursue – if they were only capable of acting on the proper insights. By ascribing interests to workers in this manner, socialist theory – as Max Weber would later show – opened the floodgates to theoretical arbitrariness: The accuracy of the knowledge that would enable the workers to arrive at the interests ascribed to them is determined entirely by the criteria with which the theory had previously disclosed social reality. Already in the works of the Saint-Simonists and other representatives of early socialism, socialist theory was in danger of becoming self-referential by projecting onto social reality a collective movement which was meant to justify its own prognoses, but which had in fact merely been constructed by ascribing certain interests to workers.

This tendency to draw self-referential conclusions shows up even more strongly in the works of Karl Marx. In nearly all of his writings, we can see the various ways he assumes an objective interest to which his own analyses merely lend expression. It is only in his historical and political writings that he seems to take account of the concrete desires of social groups enough to avoid the danger of ascribing a unified interest to all members of the working class.[19] In his early, anthropological writings, Marx proceeds in an entirely different, purely descriptive manner, by conceiving of the proletariat in its entirety as the unified subject which lends expression to the urgent desire of all human beings for self-realization. According to Marx, wage-workers are the only collective in capitalism which represent the deep-seated interest of human beings to objectify and confirm themselves in the product of their activity, and who therefore recognize their current alienation from their own natural desires.[20] When Marx turns to his economic analysis of capitalism in 1850, he changes his justification for assuming such a collective proletarian interest, while still claiming it to be necessarily revolutionary. Now the members of the working class no longer desire the abolition of capitalist private property because they sense the telos of all human nature, but because their systematic exploitation compels them to secure their very economic survival.[21] In both his early and later writings, Marx assumes that the aims of his own theory are already shared by a collective subject within social reality – a subject that, despite all the differences between the concrete feelings of the individual members, possesses a shared interest in revolution. As a consequence of this highly dubious methodological presupposition, socialist theory would henceforth be bound to the virtually transcendent precondition of an already present social movement, even though it was necessarily unclear whether it actually existed in social reality.

In Marx's theory, therefore, all the socialist concepts brought forth in the first half of the nineteenth century were declared to be the intellectual product of a revolutionary working class whose actual constitution and interests necessitated no further consideration. This method of rational ascription made a revolutionary working class a necessary component of all capitalist societies, obviating any empirical concerns. As long as social reality offered sufficient evidence to firmly support the notion of such an imaginary collective, there was no reason to doubt that socialist theory was indeed an expression or reflection of the consciousness of the working class. Even to the first representatives of German social democracy, the belief that their own interests merely mirrored the interests of all wage-workers seemed too unshakeable for there to be any reason to doubt it. We must credit the early Frankfurt School under the direction of Max Horkheimer with being the first to present empirically founded doubts in the sociological fiction of a revolutionary working class. At any rate, the interdisciplinary studies on the "authoritarianism" of the working class set a process in motion which led to the insight that there is no automatic connection between a class-specific objective situation and certain desires or interests.[22] After World War II, when in the capitalist countries of the West the situation of the working class rapidly began to change and white-collar workers began to dominate the labor market, giving rise to the term "post-industrial society",[23] there was no longer any certainty about the class affiliation of socialism. Once the revolutionary proletariat disappeared and the industrial working class had become a minority among wage-workers, it became impossible to view socialist ideals as the intellectual expression of an already existing revolutionary subject.[24]

However, the true dimensions of this problem often went unrecognized. In the eyes of its early proponents, socialism was always more than one political theory among others, comparable to liberalism; it was regarded as a future-oriented theory which would help realize an interest already present in society by activating and correcting that interest with visions of social freedom. But if such a pre-theoretical interest could no longer be presupposed given the lack of even the weakest empirical evidence, then socialism necessarily faced the danger of losing its right to exist along with its ties to a social movement. Without any link to active social forces, socialism would become just one more normative theory about a reality which fails to live up to the theory's ideal. Therefore, the corrosion of the workers' movement was more than a mere hitch; as soon as the hope was dashed that the proletariat might embody at least a fragment of the interest in revolutionary change once ascribed to it, socialism was struck to the core, for it could no longer claim to be the theoretical expression of a living movement.[25] Given this historical situation, socialism was faced with the alternative of either accepting its demotion to a purely normative theory or searching for its lost ties to the workers' movement. In the first case, it would have to follow the well-trodden path of deriving abstract principles of justice from its own ideals in order to defend these principles against competing theories.[26] In the second case, socialism had to find an interest within society which shared socialism's own aims enough to make them immune to the contingent ups and downs of other social movements. Before I return to these two alternatives in the next chapter, I still need to address the third socio-theoretical topic which, at a very early stage, began to develop into a problematic burden for socialism.

3. The assumption of a revolutionary subject longing to realize the ideals of socialism in capitalism is nearly always accompanied by the historico-philosophical assumption that capitalist relations of production will necessarily dissolve in the near future. The problem with this premise, the third burden of socialism, was not that it spurred on investigations into the self-destructive forces of capitalism, but that its conception of a clear developmental process abrogated any experimental treatment of historical processes and potentials. Here again, Saint-Simon was the first to formulate this conception; his adherents then adopted the idea from Turgot and Condorcet[27] that human history necessarily follows a course of constant progress, driven upward by continuing advances in the fields of science and technology and compelling social improvements.[28] The Saint-Simonists thus interpreted post-revolutionary

France as an epoch of so-called "critical" stagnation in which the abundant possibilities offered by the industrial mode of production could not be used to benefit all of society, because the traditional property order bestowed the power to shape society onto an idle class. Therefore, the next step in the historical process would have to consist in transferring the unearned wealth of the idle classes – the bourgeoisie, the nobility, and the church – to a state-owned central bank which would ensure the economic preconditions for the grand cooperative community of all industrial workers.[29]

However, not all contemporary authors who dabbled in socialist ideas shared the Saint-Simonists' model of historical progress. As early socialists became more involved in political activities or constructed alternative economic models (e.g. Robert Owen), they engaged less in bold speculation about the course of history. But the majority of early socialists agree with the Saint-Simonists that their own intellectual activities represented necessary steps in a ceaseless process of human progress. They viewed socialism as the result of knowledge about the inevitable developmental process leading to the abolition of competition on the market and the establishment of a cooperative association of all workers. We can find elements of such a philosophy of history in the work of Louis Blanc as well, one of the more moderate representatives of the new movement. Inspired by Condorcet and Saint-Simon, whom he admired throughout his life, Blanc assumed that the continuous progress of scientific enlightenment would sooner or later compel the very reforms he proposed in his own programmatic writings on an economic community of solidarity.[30] While this once again demonstrates the degree to which early French socialists identified with the historical optimism of enlightenment thinkers, for whom scientific knowledge represented the motor of human progress, Proudhon's thought testified to the influence of Hegel's philosophy of history. No less than his fellow socialists, Proudhon viewed socialism as the harbinger of a future social order towards which human history was necessarily progressing; but unlike other representatives of the French socialist movement, Proudhon did not claim this historical necessity to be the result of scientific progress, but rather the outcome of a gradual process in which antagonistic classes are continuously reconciled.[31] By alluding to the role of class conflicts in social progress, Proudhon, a master in the art of synthesizing the most disparate intellectual traditions, laid the groundwork for Marx's philosophy of history. Although Marx would later deny that this French anarchist had any influence on his own work, even writing a harsh criticism of Proudhon,[32] we do find traces of Proudhon's speculative thoughts in Marx's historical materialism.

However, Karl Marx presents two very different versions of the notion of necessary progress so characteristic of early socialism.[33] The first approach, which is clearly influenced by the works of Hegel and Proudhon, locates the motor of social development in a struggle between social classes which leads to continuous improvement, for at each stage the interests of the larger, but previously excluded group, prevail. Socialism represents for Marx the latest stage in the progression brought about by these struggles, as the oppressed proletariat, which represents the majority of the population, thereby attains the power to shape all of society.[34] The second approach claims a linear process of increasing scientific knowledge, which suggests a certain continuity with the ideas of Saint-Simonists. In this second model, Marx assumes that the motor of social development consists in humans' constantly increasing ability to control nature, thereby unlocking its unexploited potential and gradually compelling the reorganization of society. This leads to an entirely different kind of necessary progress in which backward and inert relations of production must be continually revolutionized in order to reconcile them with the state of the productive forces.[35] The most convincing interpretation of this version of historical materialism is provided by Gerald Cohen,[36] who refers to it as a kind of technological determinism.

Despite all the differences between these two explanatory models – the development of productive forces versus the class struggle – both assume that the "socialist" mode of production represents the next, imminent stage of history which would resolve the contradictions of capitalism. The actions of those involved play a secondary role, as they merely represent an expression of historical necessity that will prevail "behind the backs" and thus without the explicit knowledge of the actors. Of course, there have always been attempts in the Marxist tradition to weaken or qualify the role of this concept in historical materialism as a response to a number of obvious objections. The representatives of Critical Theory, for instance, proposed that we interpret Marx as stating that historical progress is only inevitable as long as social relations of production are reproduced in a "natural" way, removed from the rational control of humans.[37] Yet this sophisticated, historically limited version of historical inevitability

45

is not what prevailed in nineteenth-century socialism. From the very beginning, starting with Saint-Simon's scientific optimism and strengthened by Marx's rapidly popularized conception of history, socialists maintained that their own visions of a cooperative community of free producers merely lent expression to the aim which all of history, due to its own progressive dynamic, was inevitably striving to attain.

The problem with this determinist conception of historical progress is not only that it encouraged a kind of political complacency [*Attentismus*] soon to become a matter of major discussion within the movement;[38] rather, many of the early twentieth-century debates between social democrats and communists over how to interpret Marx's claims about the inevitability of historical progress and about whether this notion should be replaced with an ethic of transformational action bear witness to the confusion caused by the historical-philosophical determinism of socialist pioneers.[39] Even worse, the notion of inevitable historical progress would prevent socialists from perceiving historical development as a constantly changing set of challenges whose potential for social improvements needs to be discovered experimentally. By assuming historical inevitability, as John Dewey would later remark matter-of-factly,[40] socialists robbed themselves of the chance to view themselves as a movement whose best way of realizing the idea of social freedom under given historical conditions was to experiment socially. Instead, all representatives of socialism were convinced that they already knew what the new social organization of freedom would look like without ever having to explore the opportunities for change offered by rapidly changing circumstances.

Regardless of whether socialists favored reform or revolution, both sides excluded experimentation as a historical-practical method. Even those who assumed that socialist organizational principles could only be established gradually were not content to experiment with various possibilities and potentials, but pretended to possess total certainty. The divide between socialism and an experimental understanding of historical action was categorical and not gradual: Due to socialists' belief in the inevitable course of history, they were certain right from the start about the next step of social change, obviating any need for situational experimentation with various possibilities of social organization.

The strongest evidence of such incapacity for historical experimentalism can be found in the sphere in which socialist ideas were to be almost exclusively realized. In terms of how to socially shape economic relations, it was soon agreed – by Marx's arrival at the latest – that the market could only be replaced by a planned economy, which left no room for institutional mediation or a reassessment of priorities. For decades to come, this self-imposed theoretical handicap, caused by assuming a fixed course of historical progress, deprived socialism of the chance to explore and experiment with different strategies for realizing social freedom in the economic sphere. Just like their opponents in mainstream economic theory, socialists had no doubt about what more appropriate institutions of generating social wealth would look like. Like mainstream economics and its dogma of a market "free" from all political influence, socialism also restricts itself – at least in the popular imagination – to a centralized planned economy as the only viable alternative to the capitalist market economy.

If we take a closer look at the three basic conceptual assumptions I have shown to be the inherited burdens of socialism, we will see that they are entirely bound to the intellectual and social conditions of early capitalist modernization. Even the first premise, the socialist conception of society and history, clearly illustrates how socialism derives its conception of a desirable order for all future societies from a unique historical constellation. The only plausible explanation for their belief that it would no longer be necessary to democratically negotiate social aims, and that the task of social integration could be left up entirely to the unified will of cooperative producers, is that they were seduced by the enormous dynamism of early industrialization into presuming that the sources of political steering lie solely in the organizational might of industrialism. The misguided notion that individual liberties would no longer be needed in the future was therefore the price that early socialists paid for their unquestioning belief in the all-encompassing integrative power of social labor. The same is true of socialism's second problematic basic assumption, which we saw in the points of agreement between socialists from Saint-Simon to Marx. Their belief that the capitalist system necessarily entails an internal opponent upon which the socialist movement could rely – a revolutionary proletariat – only makes sense against the background of early, reckless industrialization. At this time, prior to social legislation and voting rights, it could appear for a brief moment as if the forced exploitation, wage reductions and the constant threat of unemployment facing industrial workers would necessarily unify the working class, making a unified interest in abolishing capitalism inevitable. But everything that came after, roughly summarized in the term *Verbürgerlichung* [literally: the process of becoming bourgeois], refuted this prognosis and thus also the assumption that the working class shared a revolutionary interest. This same dependence on the conditions of the industrial revolution can also be seen in the third premise of early socialist social theory, i.e. the historical inevitability of human progress. Here, however, it is not the socio-economic but the intellectual constellation of the time that comes to the fore. The historical image painted by the Saint-Simonists, Louis Blanc and Karl Marx draw largely on the spirit of progress typical of the early enlightenment era, in which hopes about the benefits of science and technology often led to claims about the inevitable progress of humankind.[41] In early socialist thought leading up to the doctrine of historical materialism, this optimistic philosophy of history would assert itself 50 years later in the conviction that the "socialist" organization of society was inevitable and imminent.

It is relatively clear today that socialism's ties to the spirit and the social conditions of the Industrial Revolution are presumably the cause for its rapid and silent decline soon after the end of World War II. As soon as social conditions were radically changed by technological advance, structural transformation, and political reforms in the 1960s and 1970s, first-generation socialist ideas were bound to become less attractive given that their socio-theoretical content remained anchored in the early nineteenth century. Every attempt to revive these old ideas thus had to begin with the hard work of gradually unraveling their entanglement in the basic socio-theoretical assumptions of socialism, all of which had been refuted by the course of events, in order to make room for a more adequate contemporary articulation. Only if the original vision of social freedom can be articulated in a theory of society and history that lives up to contemporary reality will it be able to regain a piece of its earlier vitality. Yet we must be cautious, for we cannot merely abandon these three faulty premises. Because they represent necessary elements of a theory that seeks to motivate future action, we must find a theoretical substitute for these premises at a higher level of abstraction, detached from the spirit of industrialization. In the next two chapters, I will make some initial proposals for how to reformulate these premises. In the first step, I will discuss the socialist critique of the capitalist market economy and present a socialist understanding of history that enables us to retain confidence in the realizability of socialist demands for improvement, while abstaining from any belief in historical inevitability (chapter III). In the concluding chapter, I will sketch how socialism's understanding of society, and thus the entire horizon of this project, will have to be altered if it is to take account, after so many years of hesitation, of the functional differentiation of modern societies (chapter IV).

III

Paths of Renewal (1): Socialism as Historical Experimentalism

This chapter begins with a brief summary of the results of the previous chapters in order to assess the challenges facing the renewal of socialism today. If we were to summarize the constitutive features of this movement in a single sentence, we would be forced to resort to a paradoxical formulation: The theoretical framework within which socialism develops the fruitful and far-reaching idea of resolving the contradictory legacy of the French Revolution by institutionalizing social freedoms owes the entirety of its experiences to the Industrial Revolution. To express this paradox more clearly, we could borrow an idea from Marx and say that in socialism, the normative force of the idea of social freedom is prevented from unfolding its true potential by a theoretical framework stemming from the Industrial Revolution. The theorists of the original socialist movement were unable to unleash the potential of their practical and political intention to establish modern society as a community of cooperative subjects – an aim that extended far beyond their day – due to the fact that they had bound themselves to the conceptual premises of Manchester capitalism.

Similar diagnoses of socialism's basic flaw were made by sympathetic critics after the end of World War II at the latest. Here I am referring primarily to the postwar French journal *Socialisme ou barbarie*, whose most notable contributor was Cornelius Castoriadis.[1] But we can also count Habermas' attempt immediately after the fall of the Berlin Wall to preserve the core of socialism as an effort to revive the original idea of the movement.[2] Unlike so-called "analytical Marxism", which attempted to rid itself of the above-mentioned problems by presenting socialism as a purely normative alternative to liberal theories of justice,[3] the tradition exemplified by Castoriadis and Habermas retains the thought that socialism must reflect on its own conditions of possibility and aim to bring about an alternative life-form. Socialism wants to offer much more than an improved conception of social justice or a convincing justification of a moral imperative; by conceiving of itself as a movement directed toward the future, socialism necessarily aims to make modern society more "social" in the full sense of the term by unleashing forces or potentials already contained in the current society. Whoever fully understands the challenge facing the attempt to revive socialism today is also faced with a number of intractable problems deriving from the roots of the movement in early industrialism. A more universalizable substitute must be found for all of its misleading assumptions about history and social theory, for we cannot merely adopt the idea of establishing social freedoms, nor the notion of a movement already present in society, nor the assumption that a historical tendency supports our own intentions. Instead, we need to find a complement for all three of these basic assumptions, thereby making socialism a theory aimed at bringing about practical change. We need complementary ideas that correspond to the more advanced consciousness of our time. Therefore, if socialism is to have a future, it must be revived in a post-Marxist form.

This roughly constitutes the task of the following chapters. The aim is to formulate the individual elements of the historical and social theories of classic socialism in a more abstract fashion, thus making them more relevant to the present. This will in turn make it appear more justified and historically possible to focus our unified powers on expanding social rather than individual freedoms. However, I can no longer proceed as I have in my account of the three building blocks of socialist social theory in chapter II. In order to find solutions at a more abstract level, I will have to move back and forth between the various basic assumptions of socialism, because often I can only make corrections in one place by making corrections in another. In my attempt to create an image of society and history that would do service to socialism, therefore, everything is related to everything. None of the premises upon which its traditional background conceptions rely can be changed without also changing the others.

Nevertheless, when it comes to updating socialism theoretically, it makes sense to begin at the same point at which I began my reconstruction of its socio-theoretical premises. After all, finding the institutional location of social freedom within modern society represents the crucial point when it comes to the practice of the original socialist movement. As we have seen, early socialist thinkers were all convinced that the social cause for a merely individualized understanding of freedom, and thus for the divide within the legitimacy of the new liberal order, lies in the behavioral constraints of an economic system which compels subjects to merely pursue their own interests and to view their partners in interaction solely as competitors. Although early socialists were not yet sure how to understand the early stages of the market economy – Marx's analysis of capitalism would later clear things up to a certain extent[4] – they all saw the need to overcome economic individualism if there was to be any chance of reconciling freedom and fraternity, and thus of realizing the "sociality" [*Sozialwerden*] of society. This equating of fraternity with a transformed economic system, of social freedom with a cooperative economy is the reason that socialism would almost immediately be regarded – by socialists and non-socialists alike – as a purely economic project. Because the socialist movement was largely convinced that the forces of increasing desocialization and individualization were rooted completely in the new capitalist economic order, they felt they only needed to replace individual freedom with social freedom in this one place in order to fulfill all the necessary prerequisites for relations of solidarity among the members of society. This conclusion, characteristic of traditional socialism as a whole, must be revised in two different ways if the socialist cause is to be made fruitful for the present. The first revision concerns the thoughts of early socialists on the reconstruction of the economic system (1). The second revision concerns the manner in which they conceive of the freedoms of a future fraternal society solely in terms of social freedom within the economic sphere (2). I will deal with the first of these revisions in the present chapter, leaving the question of the shape of freedom in a future, "socialist" society for the concluding chapter. In the course of my argumentation, we will see that corrections within the economic core of original socialism will also entail making changes to its other two theoretical premises, i.e. to its concept of history and its underlying model of society.

With a bit of hermeneutic goodwill, we could say that the very first socialists understood their conceptions of an alternative economic order as experimental explorations of the possibilities opened up by the new medium of the market when it came to expanding relationships of solidarity and cooperation. Owen's cooperatives, as well as the – largely French – plans to ensure fair distribution of starting capital primarily to the benefit of the lower classes, were mainly intended to allow the working masses – by means of self-managed cooperatives – to become strong participants in a market restricted by price regulations and legal guidelines. We could call these efforts "market socialist", to use a much later term; all of these measures were meant to satisfy the preconditions for social freedom in the economic sphere.[5] This might seem somewhat naïve given the force and the brutality with which owners of capital were already pursuing their profit interests at the time; however, it not only displayed the charm of a bold beginning, but also had the advantage of representing a kind of "learning by doing". Those involved were not entirely aware of the kind of economic system they were dealing with in their intellectual activities. Despite their boundless faith in the necessary march of history towards socialism, they were forced to explore the extent of the moral tolerance of the market. Marx was the first to put an end to this "experimental" early socialist approach. This young exile was convinced that the market represented an entire ensemble of social relationships that could not be split up into individual segments on the basis of certain moral conceptions. Marx, by far the most talented economist among the early socialists, saw the essential elements of this new social formation as consisting – alongside the law of supply and demand, which governed exchange relations in the market – in private capitalist ownership of the means of production, on the one hand, and the fundamental propertylessness of the proletariat, whose labor created value, on the other. These three elements created in his eyes an indissoluble unity, a "totality" in the Hegelian sense, for which he had already begun to use the term "capitalism" even in his early writings. Only occasionally does Marx's work seem to allow for the possibility that the capitalist market is not a fixed entity, but a constantly changing and changeable set of institutions whose reformability was to be tested through repeated experiments.[6]

For the most part, however, Marx's conceptual approach – in the tradition of Hegelian thinking in terms of totality – identifies the various features of the market so strongly with capitalism that even long after his death, it was impossible for socialists to conceive of an alternative, socialist economic system that did not rid itself of all market elements. And because the only model for such an economy was the centrally planned economy, they were even forced to conceive of the new economic order as a vertical relationship with all actors on the one side and a superior authority on the other, even though according to the original socialist intuition the producers should relate to each other horizontally. As valuable as Marx's analysis of capitalism was to the socialist movement, having provided it with a systematic economic theory which would henceforth compete with classical economics, the totalizing features of this theory represented a great disadvantage. His conception of capitalism as a unified social system, in which the imperatives of the market compel it to constantly expand, robbed socialists of any chance of conceiving of economic collectivization other than in the form of a centralized planned economy.

Today, the capitalist market certainly appears to correspond precisely to the developmental tendencies Marx had foreseen. The old industrial proletariat and the new service proletariat have lost any prospect of long-term employment in secure jobs, while profits appear higher than ever, leading to an enormous increase in income disparity between the wealthy few and the larger masses. Furthermore, ever more public sectors are being subjected to the principle of profitability, such that Marx's prognosis of a "real subsumption" of all sectors of social life under capital seems gradually to be coming true.[7] However, this was not always the case in the capitalist market society, nor must it always remain that way. The most important task when it comes to reviving the socialist tradition consists in revising Marx's equating of the market economy with capitalism, thereby opening up space for alternative uses of the market. If we think back to the original intuition of socialism, according to which the promises of the French Revolution were to be realized by institutionalizing social freedom in the economic sphere, then there are three economic models for realizing such horizontal cooperation and mutual supplementation. First of all, there is the market as Adam Smith conceived of it when he interpreted the law of supply and demand as operating according to the mechanism of an "invisible hand" through which the economic interests of equal and benevolent citizens complement each other.[8] Then there is the noble vision of an "association of free producers", in which the working members of a community independently organize and manage their economic affairs by means of a democratically self-governing civil society. Finally, we can conceive of the exercise of social freedom in the economic sphere as a way in which citizens engage in democratic will-formation and assign to the government the task of steering and supervising the process of economic reproduction in the interest of the well-being of society.[9] None of these models deserves to be merely pushed aside by a fundamentally revised version of socialism. On the contrary, because they all share the elementary notion that cooperating workers should determine the allocation of the means for satisfying generally shared needs on the basis of equal opportunities for participation, these models must be regarded in the first instance as equally valuable alternatives to the capitalist market. Of course, we must not forget that Smith originally sought to characterize the market as an economic institution in which self-interested subjects show a benevolent attitude toward the justified interests of others.[10] However, if all three models represent equally worthy candidates for institutionally implementing social freedom within the economic sphere, then there can be no apodictic predetermination immune to examination. Instead, a renewed version of socialism would have to leave it up to experimentation whether the market, civil society or the democratic constitutional state represents the most appropriate steering principle when it comes to realizing social freedom in the economic sphere. Before I can pursue this economic line of argumentation any further, I must fundamentally revise the second building bloc of classical socialism, because the idea of expanding the space of social freedom in the economic sphere by experimenting with more appropriate forms of institutional implementation cannot be reconciled with the notion – shared by all socialists from Saint-Simon to Marx – of necessary human progress.

As was already briefly mentioned in chapter II, John Dewey accused traditional socialism of being incapable of taking up an experimental stance towards historical processes of transformation. Dewey argued that if we assume the next stage of historical development to be already clear; if we are certain that the capitalist socialist formation will necessarily be followed by a certain socialist order, then there will no longer be any need to explore already existing potentials and find out which measures are most appropriate for attaining the desired transformation.[11] This objection has more than a merely corrective function; it is more fundamental in that it directs our attention to the basic irreconcilability between the assumption of historical necessity and the intellectual method of experimenting with opportunities for specific changes. We must understand statements about certain desired steps of social progress either as the result of objective insights into the laws of history or as the result of the practical exploration of situationally-dependent possibilities for specific changes. However, such an experimental understanding of history, according to which each step of the historical process contains new potentials for change that need to be unlocked, demands a criterion for determining what can count as an improvement in a concrete situation. We can only regard a given social fact as representing "potential" if we have already given at least a vague definition of what this fact could be good for.

At this point John Dewey operates with a speculative conception which bears a distant resemblance to Hegel. Surprisingly, however, it is so closely related to the original socialist idea of social freedom that it gives us a first indication of a solution to the problem that arises here. According to Dewey, the normative guideline in the experimental search for the most comprehensive answer to a socially problematic situation must be thought of as the removal of barriers to free communication among the members of society so that problems can be solved in the most intelligent fashion.[12] Dewey argued for the superiority of such a cooperative and socially free solution to problematic situations by delving deep into the realm of the philosophy of nature; his argument therefore reveals something about the kind of evolutionary force upon which a revised version of socialism could rely if it wishes to be an expression not of a moral imperative but of a historical tendency. The starting point for Dewey's far-reaching considerations consists in his claim that "associational" or "communal" behavior constitutes a basic feature of all things; therefore, as history unfolds, potentials are unleashed and realized by the establishment of connections between hitherto isolated "individual things". It is only if the latter begin to communicate with each other that the future possibilities not yet revealed in these phenomena can be uncovered. The tendency of all reality to uncover such possibilities through the "interaction" of different elements, and thus its tendency to create new realities, takes place at all stages of reality, spanning from the physical to the organic all the way up to the "mental". For Dewey, the highest stage in this hierarchy of reality is the "social", for here the wealth and subtlety of these possibilities is additionally augmented by "specifically human forms of grouping".[13] Now, at the evolutionary stage of the social, the basically interactive character of all reality takes on the particular quality of meaningful communication, infusing previously unleashed potentials with additional meaning and thus enabling them to multiply. Even at this highest stage of reality, however, Dewey argues that the more potentials we unleash and realize, the more freely the individual elements will be able to interact with each other. This moves Dewey to conclude that within the reality of human communities, possibilities can only be completely realized if all members are able to participate as freely as possible in the kind of meaningful communication that is typical of such communities.

According to Dewey, there is another cause for the fact that this basic feature of the "social", free communication between members of society, actually represents a "force" in social reality and thus brings forth a historical tendency. In his eyes, every group excluded from interaction will eventually seek to be included in the social process of communication, for isolation always entails an internal loss of freedom, a stagnation of prosperity and growth. From Dewey's perspective, therefore, the periodic revolts of social groups against their exclusion from social interaction ensure that the free and unlimited communication underlying the social gradually becomes

reality in the social life-world.[14] Dewey therefore gives
a methodological response to the question as to the
criterion for the experimental exploration of appropriate solutions to problematic situations. The more those
who are affected by a problem are involved in the search
for solutions to that problem, the more such historical-
social experiments will lead to better and more stable
solutions. Whenever barriers to communication are
removed, the ability of the community to perceive as
many of the currently hidden potentials for solving a
problem productively will grow. If, for illustrative purposes, we were to translate this methodological notion
into the terminology of Hegel's philosophy of objective
spirit, we could say that we can measure progress within
the social sphere only in terms of whether the bearers of
that progress – the inter-related subjects – are freed from
dependencies and merely external, negative determina-
tions. If a transformation in the institutional makeup of
a society meets this condition, thus bringing about an
emancipation from restrictions to equal participation in
the self-creation of society, then according to Hegel it
can count as a stage in the process of the comprehensive
realization of freedom.[15] We could therefore say that
for Hegel as well, "improvements" within the sphere of
the social result from the gradual overcoming of barriers to free communication among members of society,
who aim to rationally explore and lay down rules for
their shared existence. When it comes to replacing
the hitherto dominant faith in the necessity of historical progress within socialism with a kind of historical
experimentalism, these seemingly far-off considerations
are more fruitful than might appear at first sight. The
conception shared by both Dewey and Hegel, accord-

ing to which the only criterion for social improvement consists in the liberation from barriers to communication and from dependencies that prevent interaction, provides us with a theoretical instrument for casting the idea of social freedom both as a historical foundation and as a criterion for an experimental understanding of socialism.[16]

In order to make this seemingly odd claim more plausible, a brief reminder of the historical understanding of early socialism is needed. As we saw, these socialists understood their own future-oriented theory as an expression of the inevitable progress of human productive forces or of the equally necessary advance of contemporary class struggles. In both cases, the proletariat was regarded as the social representative of the consciousness of a necessary transition to a higher and historically appropriate social formation. Early socialists thus ascribed to the proletariat an objective interest in these same changes. Yet after both of these background certainties – the necessity of historical progress and a revolutionary proletariat – had collapsed and become obvious intellectual fictions of the age of the Industrial Revolution, socialism was in danger of losing all anchoring in a progressive historical tendency that lent social grounding to its demands. Therefore, it was and is in danger of degenerating into merely one theory of justice among others, turning its demands into mere normative demands rather than the expression of already existing demands.[17] In order to avoid this dilemma, which would basically spell the downfall of socialism as a theory which sees itself as the expression of a historical tendency, we need to find an alternative form of historical anchoring. Those socialists who believe they can abstain from such anchoring, presuming it to entail nothing but unneeded speculation, have already conceded that our future political and moral self-understanding can get along without any socialist vision at all. With regard to the alternative, however, I believe that the above-mentioned considerations presented by John Dewey (and Hegel) represent the best chance for socialism to regain – at a higher level of abstraction – the force that an anchoring in the historical process can provide to their own demands. This notion is based on the presumption of a strong resemblance between, on the one hand, Dewey's claim that all of human history is marked by the gradual expansion of communication and social interaction, and, on the other hand, the notion that early socialists believed they could apply to the economic sphere. The latter's intention to remove all obstructions to the realization of all three principles of the French Revolution by creating conditions of social freedom in the economic sphere is ultimately based on the same concept. They also aimed to overcome the opposition between individual freedom and solidarity, which they experienced as a normative limitation, by further expanding social communication. The thinker who had the strongest sense that the socialist movement represented an attempt to continue the task of removing barriers to social communication – a task which determines all of history – was Proudhon, influenced in turn by Hegel. At one point in Proudhon's work, he writes – in line with Dewey – that the force of all historical development, indeed of all living growth, consists in the tendency to realize reciprocity to an ever greater extent.[18]

If we base socialism on such a historical self-understanding, then it can no longer be viewed as the articulated consciousness of social changes that are in turn the necessary consequence of the already advanced potential of the productive forces that cannot adequately develop under given social circumstances. Nor can we view it, as Marx occasionally did, as the reflexive organ of the most advanced stage of the class struggle, as long as we view the latter as a succession of necessary conflicts between collectives with seemingly fixed interests. Instead, socialism must be viewed as the specific modern articulation of the fact that in the course of history and on the basis of varying social circumstances, new groups constantly seek to draw public attention to their own demands by attempting to tear down barriers to communication and thereby expand the space of social freedom. Such a "struggle" certainly characterizes the entirety of human history and continues even today; after all, in the course of the expansion of social interaction and the increase of political connections, new collectives are repeatedly faced with a lack of recognition for their concerns. In each case, the only possibility for attaining such recognition is to invoke already implicitly accepted norms and thereby to demand the right to have a say in the formulation of social rules, thus removing another barrier to social communication. If socialism wishes to engage in such a struggle for recognition, then it must view its own origin as the moment in which – within the modern social order confirmed normatively by the French Revolution – it became apparent that the justified needs of the working population could only be satisfied by tearing down barriers to communication in the economic sphere. The private capitalist organization of the market proved to be the social institution that prevented certain segments of the population from equally profiting from the overcoming of hitherto dominant dependencies and unrecognized heteronomy. However, socialism could not remain tied to this moment in time if it truly understood itself as a reflexive authority that points to the power of social communication throughout human history. Because modern society necessarily erects new barriers for ever different groups, thus preventing them from taking advantage of the institutionalized promises of liberty, equality and fraternity, socialism has had to progress along with the resulting struggles in order to be an advocate for victims' demand to be included in social communication. The demand for the "social" contained in the very term "socialism" represents the general desire to remove all social hindrances to the exercise of freedom in solidarity. As long as this aim has not been attained – an aim which represents more than a mere moral demand, as it expresses the definitive structural principle of the social[19] – this understanding of socialism will not lose its right to exist. It will be the representative of the demands of the social in a society in which one-sided interpretations of basic principles of legitimacy constantly allow the domination of merely private interests under the guise of individual freedom, thus also permitting violations of the promise of solidarity.

Before I proceed to draw the consequences of this expanded understanding of socialism for its original idea of social freedom, I must first pick up where I left off before my digression on the historical status of the "social". We saw that given the disappearance of socialists' belief in its inevitable victory, it is no longer clear how social freedom should best be realized in the economic sphere. This question can only be answered by means of experimentation, by exploring different ideas whose sole commonality consists in pointing up possibilities for economic value-creation beyond capitalism as a cooperative process aided by various institutional mechanisms. This exploratory process in no way excludes the possibility that based on the insights we gradually gain and depending on the needs we wish to satisfy, it might prove advisable to consider different models of economic action and therefore to test out the possibility of mixed economic systems. The guideline for any experimentation with different economic combinations must lie in strengthening "the social" in the economic sphere as much as possible, enabling all those involved to satisfy their needs through complementary activity without compulsion or restricted influence.

However, this type of socialism must realize that it can only hope to find support for such experiments to the degree that it can convincingly show the capitalist economic system to be capable of fundamental change and even revolution. Therefore, the natural enemy of socialism – today just as in Marx's day – is the predominant school of economic theory, which has sought for over 200 years to justify the capitalist market as the only efficient means for coordinating economic action under the conditions of an expanding population and its growing needs. One of socialists' most urgent tasks therefore consists in cleansing the concept of the market from all subsequent capitalist additives in order to examine its own moral sustainability.[20] This kind of project, already initiated by authors such as Karl Polanyi, Amitai Etzioni and Albert Hirschman,[21] must begin by distinguishing between various markets according to the respective goods exchanged there. Here we need to examine whether supply and demand is a suitable method for determining prices on all these markets, or whether this has a detrimental effect on much more important needs. The deconstruction of the market ideology must go further, however, for it is not self-evident that the mere ownership of the means of production should justify a claim to profit. After all, the exponential growth of profits cannot be sufficiently explained by the owner's own labor. Here we could draw on Friedrich Kambartel's conceptual efforts to prove that the basis for the legitimacy of the market is irreconcilable with capital rents and profits by speculation.[22] Such philosophical studies on the conceptual arsenal employed by standard economic theory show in general how vague the category of "economic efficiency" is when it comes to justifying capitalist markets. Optimal gains on capital, a purely quantitative expression, is thereby implicitly equated with a qualitative understanding of productivity leading to an increase in the well-being of all of society.[23] All these deconstructions of the dominant economic theory seek to undermine the deep-seated impression that markets require the inheritable private ownership of the means of production in order to function, and thus can only function in a capitalist form. If we push this process of disenchanting a bit further, we would be likely to come across a number of other features of the market that turn out to be merely artificial additions made by interested parties in order to legitimate the market in its current form. Why, for instance, should the labor market necessarily be understood as a system of incentives, if it remains psychologically unclear whether the prospect of an increase in income truly motivates people to perform more and better?[24] Or why should the financial markets allow speculative profits on derivatives trading, if it clearly does not benefit the real economy and does nothing for the well-being of society?

It is absolutely imperative that a revised form of socialism pose such questions, since it can no longer be so certain about how to best realize its aim of realizing social freedom in the economic sphere. The institution of the market must be broken down into its disparate and separable components so that we can re-examine how suitable they are for cooperative forms of economic coordination given the complexity of individual needs. In the course of this examination, nothing can be excluded as being obviously wrong, not even objections to the right of succession or the possibility of common ownership among producers.[25] Such thought experiments, however, can only be useful to a revised socialism to the degree that they can truly be understood as specific explorations of the possibilities for expanding social freedom in the economic sphere. And if we must fundamentally exclude any certainty about the final state of a socialist economy, then we cannot take this abstention from certainty so far as to cause us to lose sight of the outlines of our aim or "end in view", as John Dewey once put it.[26] When it comes to experimenting with institutional models, we must welcome all proposals that are somehow committed to freeing producers from constraints and dependencies, thus enabling them to view themselves as free contributors to the task of equally satisfying the needs of all members of society, a task that can only be fulfilled in reciprocity.

Just as was the case a century ago, when the desirability and possibility of "nationalizing" or "socializing" private ownership of the means of production was an issue of heated debate,[27] the decisive question remains whether the gradual emancipation of workers can only be achieved by the expropriation of private property or whether this emancipation is reconcilable with existing forms of ownership, for example by marginalizing private ownership in specific sectors of the economy. There are a number of experimental models for both market-socialist conceptions and for ideas of "socializing" the market from below by introducing a guaranteed minimum income and various democratic controls.[28] Deciding between these models is not merely a theoretical issue, but also requires a struggle for free spaces and social niches in which – taking account of the principle of "minimum mutilation",[29] i.e. by preserving principles that have proven themselves in practice – we can test under real conditions which alternative is most suitable for achieving our short-term goals.

The logic of historical experimentalism dictates that the more these theoretical re-combinations and preliminary designs can be tested under real economic conditions, the more weight they will have in terms of our practical and political orientations. A revised socialism, therefore, should assemble an internal archive of past attempts at economic collectivization as a kind of memory bank detailing the advantages and disadvantages of specific measures.[30] This archive should span from documents of early experiments with production and consumption collectives, a comprehensive account of the many "socialization debates" after World War I, attempts in Vienna and elsewhere to construct social housing, as well as reports on union efforts in Germany and elsewhere to "humanize labor". The more historical documents we assemble, the more comprehensive our knowledge would be about proven dead-ends and more promising paths of socially reorganizing the market.[31] Of course, experimental socialism will also have to maintain an overview of current explorations of alternative economic forms. Perhaps it would be even more appropriate to say that it would have to assign itself the task of moral advocate wherever there are possibilities of testing the expansion of social freedom within the economic sector. There are a surprising number of current economic practices in social reality that meet the requirements of such experiments under real conditions. As Erik Olin Wright has shown in his book *Envisioning Real Utopias*,[32] there are a number of economic initiatives – from the cooperatives in the Basque town of Mondragón to worker "solidarity funds" in Canada – that are committed to the spirit of experimental socialism.

As these considerations also make clear, it is misleading to regard socialism merely as the intellectual expression of the industrial working class or as the mouthpiece of an already revolutionary proletariat. The idea that socialist theory is necessarily tied to a single group was originally the result of a specious ascription of objective interests; it has meanwhile been refuted by the structural transformation of the labor market and by the dissolution of the labor movement. It would be wrong to succumb to nostalgia and desperately attempt to artificially resuscitate this idea, because the inevitable question as to who will be the bearer of a revised socialism must be answered at a higher level of abstraction. If socialism understands itself as part of a historical process of liberation from dependencies and barriers to communication, attempting to continue this process under the advanced conditions of modern societies, then it must refrain from regarding the social movement which currently represents the strongest and clearest articulation of the desire for freedom as being the sole embodiment of the basic idea of socialism. Such a fixation on individual movements, on temporary organizations of group-specific resistance, has the disadvantage of only representing a narrow segment of the diverse number of justified experiences of heteronomy and social exclusion. Moreover, the idea that socialism is obligated to "represent" already articulated interests, to be the mouthpiece of a single social movement, contradicts socialism's own intention of being the mouthpiece of countless other interests that have not yet been articulated at all.[33] The ambivalence of the notion that socialists must search for a collective bearer of their theory becomes even more obvious once we recognize that social movements owe their existence to complex and contingent circumstances that are not always capable of being understood as a whole. Such movements come and go over time and depend on the attention of the media, which tells us nothing meaningful about the actual extent of heteronomy and degrading dependency in the economic sphere. The new "service proletariat", for instance, is hardly capable of articulating shared interests due to the isolated working conditions of its members and their exclusion from all forms of public will-formation. As a result, there is no social movement that could be its political advocate; therefore, it must be regarded by socialists as an important addressee of its moral aims.[34]

All of this suggests that we need a different way of posing the inevitable question as to who represents the social bearer of socialist ideals, i.e. the social embodiment of these ideals in existing social relations. Contemporary socialism should not search for representatives of a consciousness of the new in the old (i.e. of what Hegel saw in important historical figures and Marxist socialism saw in the proletariat) at the concrete level of individual or collective subjectivities. This would put far too much emphasis on the ephemeral and the contingent in the increasingly rapid process of social transformation. Instead, we should search for the real expression of the future wherever trace elements of desired progress in the expansion of social freedoms can already be found in existing institutions, in altered legal structures and shifts in mentality that can no longer be rolled back. For socialism today, such publicly accepted breakthroughs, i.e. historical events that Kant once interpreted as "Geschichtszeichen",[35] are much more reliable indicators of the chances of socialism than even the most frequent appearances of social movements.

When it comes to the economic sphere upon which I have focused my argument, this shift in perspective would mean regarding the social legislation of the early twentieth century (e.g. the law of co-determination in West Germany, minimum wages in various countries, etc.) not merely as contingent measures, but as first steps of progress along the long and difficult path to the socialization of the labor market. If we draw an imaginary line from such institutional breakthroughs toward the future, it will become clear which further measures will be required in the near future in order to come closer to the goal of realizing social freedom in the economic sphere. However, we cannot assume that we can simply design the next steps from scratch, just as little as we could determine the final goal in advance. Instead, our aims and our means will constantly correct each other depending on the outcome of concrete experiments; and, because the latter require constant repetition, we cannot have reliable knowledge of our final goal. For this very reason, however, we cannot categorically exclude the possibility that the economic form anticipated by the socialist concept of social freedom might lead to relations that could only be termed "market socialist".

In any case, once we no longer think of social collectives but of institutional achievements as the true embodiment of the demands of socialism, then everything changes. The addressees of socialist experimental insights will no longer be the members of a certain social group, but all citizens – provided the latter are convinced that their individual freedom can only be realized through cooperation in solidarity in significant spheres of social life. The guarantee for the realizability of socialism will no longer be the existence of a social movement with corresponding aims, but the capacity to bring about institutional reforms within the given social reality – reforms that point toward future change. The more legal reforms or mental shifts that socialism can look back upon in its search for traces of its own intentions, the more it will regain confidence in the realizability of its visions in the future.

However, this account of a fundamentally revised socialism still contains a fracture – one that reveals a further discrepancy between socialism's new intentions and its original conception. It is easy to see this fracture once we realize that traditional socialism viewed the working class as the addressee of its vision, because in the future there would no longer be citizens at all. After all, socialists were convinced that all freedom would be realized in the form of economic cooperation, such that an additional sphere in which the members of society encounter each other not as producers, but as "citoyens", would no longer be needed. Therefore, when I say that socialism must address itself to all citizens, then this cannot immediately be reconciled with the original premises of socialism. I make positive reference to a process of democratic will-formation which, according to classical socialism, should eventually be abolished. This awkward tension can only be removed if the idea of social freedom can be freed from its ties to the economic sphere. This brings me to the second step of my attempt to free socialism from its own intellectual framework in order to give it renewed effect.

IV

Paths of Renewal (2): The Idea of a Democratic Form of Life

The fact that early socialists made no effort to transfer their newly acquired concept of social freedom to other social spheres remains a theoretical mystery. In chapter II, I traced this back to the fact that the founders of the socialist movement located the cause of what they called "private egotism" solely in the behavioral constraints of the capitalist market economy. They therefore believed they must direct all their political efforts toward overcoming this economic order. Incapable of even imagining the emancipatory significance of the civil liberties established by the French Revolution, these authors merely regarded them as the license to accumulate private wealth and thus as entirely dispensable in a future, socialist society. Ever since, socialism has been incapable of finding productive access to the idea of political democracy. Although socialists occasionally considered plans to establish economic democracy, workers councils and similar institutions of collective self-organization, these all applied exclusively to the economic sphere, because it was assumed that in the future there would no longer be any need for a process of ethical and political will-formation, i.e. for democratic self-government. Even the later, somewhat hastily added adjective "democratic" could not really alter socialist pioneers' crucial mistake, i.e. their economic fundamentalism, because this did not suffice to clarify the relationship between economic cooperation in social freedom and democratic will-formation. Instead, socialists merely adopted the liberal concept of democracy while leaving everything else the same, thus creating a strange hybrid that lacked any unity or conceptual coherence.[1] Once socialists began to sense the lack of democracy in their own movement, it would have been better to go back and study the writings of their founders and search for the origins of this fatal misunderstanding: The inability to adapt the groundbreaking concept of social freedom to the reality of a functionally differentiated society, making it impossible to apply this concept to gradually separated social spheres.

In order to correct this mistake, let us return to the origin of the idea of social freedom. This idea was developed by the early socialists and the young Marx with the intention of eliminating the contradiction they saw anchored in the principles of the new liberal-capitalist social order: Within the market economy, freedom consisted in unbridled individualism, which condemned the propertyless classes to poverty and thus contradicted the demand that not only "freedom", but also "fraternity" and "equality" should be realized. The idea of social freedom was thought to lead out of this impasse by offering a mechanism or scheme of action according to which the freedom of each would directly presuppose the freedom of the other. If, given the corresponding institutional preconditions, the individual aims of the members of society were so interwoven that they could only be realized through mutual affirmation and sympathy, then fraternity would become the mode for realizing freedom, thus reconciling freedom and fraternity in a community of equals. All early socialists – from Louis Blanc and Proudhon to Karl Marx – claimed that this contradiction and the fact of inequality could only be overcome by organizing a community in which the actions of free individuals supplemented each other. This would eliminate not only the opposition between freedom and fraternity, but also the distinction between rich and poor, for members of society would then regard each other as partners in interaction, to whom they owe a certain measure of solidarity for the sake of their own freedom.

But precisely at this point, a mystery begins to take shape. The fruitful model of social freedom, crucial when it comes to understanding individual freedom and solidarity as mutually dependent and no longer contradicting principles, refers exclusively to the sphere of economic action, without even considering whether it might be applicable to other spheres of the emerging society. If we leave aside the fact that a major reason for this missed opportunity lies in socialists' conviction that the evil of uninhibited individualism stems solely from the legal isolation of individuals on the market, the second, equally important reason lies in their shared links to the spirit of industrialism. The founding fathers of socialism were unable and even unwilling to take account of the process of functional differentiation occurring before their eyes, because they were all convinced that in the future the integration of all social spheres would be determined solely by the requirements of industrial production. They did so in spite of the fact that their liberal predecessors and their intellectual opponents had long since begun to take account of the socio-political consequences – arising by the late eighteenth century at the latest – of the differentiation of society into various social spheres, which came to be analyzed increasingly with reference to their respective functions.[2] In its studies of the work of Hobbes, and even more so in the works of Locke and Hume, liberalism recognized that – along with the differentiation of "morality" and "legality" – the two subsystems of "society" and the "state" needed to be distinguished, as each of these spheres seemed to function according to their own respective laws – either private and personal or public and neutral. Somewhat contrary to this first distinction, liberalism also sought to distinguish a public and general sphere from the purely private sphere, taking account of the relationships of friendship and marriage that were becoming increasingly based solely on affection. Finally, the discipline of political economy, which was still just getting off the ground, had already made great progress in terms of making a clear distinction between the economy and the state, not least to defend market transactions from political intervention.[3] Hegel reacted to these liberal differentiations and took them into account in his *Philosophy of Right*, going on to propose a way of distinguishing between different spheres of action in terms of their specific tasks. According to his theory, the law or "right" has the task of preserving the private autonomy of all individual members of society; the family is responsible for the socialization and the satisfaction of natural needs;

the market should guarantee the sufficient provision of means of subsistence; and, finally, the state is to ensure the ethical and political integration of the whole.[4] Even if early socialists largely agreed that these separations and demarcations were somewhat excessive, since they simply denied the primacy of the capitalist economy, they should have at least faced up to the theoretical challenge implied by the assumption of functional differentiation. But instead, they merely showed their utter lack of understanding for liberal and postliberal considerations, or they simply brushed them aside with a few cursory remarks, as Marx had done in his famous critique of Hegel's philosophy of right.[5]

Upon closer inspection, early socialists' failure to recognize the functional differentiation of society is due to their failure to distinguish sufficiently between the empirical and the normative level of these diagnoses. Otherwise they would have been right to object that the systematic separation of the state or private relationships from the economy did not amount to much, since both spheres continued to be dominated by economic imperatives, while still emphasizing at the same time the desirability of a functional separation between these two spheres in the future.[6] But precisely because they did not distinguish between these two levels, they immediately slipped from empirical description into normative claims. Just like pre-modern social theorists, socialists from Saint-Simon to Marx conceived of the functioning of societies as being vertically directed by a central authority. The only difference is that this authority was not represented by the state, but by the economy. It would have been far more insightful from the perspective of social theory to criticize the capitalist relations of the time for not permitting the various independent spheres of action the freedom to follow their own respective social logic – which was the freedom that representatives of liberalism originally accorded to these spheres. It would have been possible, therefore, to affirm the tendency towards functional differentiation and demand that e.g. love and democracy be excepted from economic imperatives. At the same time, socialists could have expressed their skepticism about the possibilities for establishing this separation under capitalist economic conditions. Due to socialists' incapacity to follow this path and take functional differentiation as a task rather than as a social fact, socialism ended up in an awkward relationship with the liberal tradition. Although the latter never developed its own theory of society, perhaps with the exception of Adam Smith and Max Weber, the explanatory power of liberalism could still appear superior to its socialist rivals simply because the latter failed to take account of functional differentiation.

It is this deep-seated incapacity of early socialists that helps explain their characteristic blindness to the importance of rights. Because they denied any division into various social spheres, they perceived the newly born civil liberties only where they were relevant to the central direction of the economy. This in turn meant that they necessarily lost sight of the emancipatory role these liberties play in the entirely different sphere of political will-formation.[7] The potential for overcoming barriers to communication by institutionalizing basic liberal rights thus remained closed to early socialists, even though it would have made perfect sense to employ their own concept of social freedom to explain – along with Rousseau – the anchoring of these new rights in a process of collective will-formation. If the contents of the founding documents of the French Revolution – which go back to Rousseau's Social Contract – are true, i.e. that only universal rights are legitimate and thus only deserve to be obeyed by individuals who can agree to them in principle, then this obviously requires debate and consideration not only on the part of isolated individuals, but as a collective of mutually supplementing individuals.[8] It would have been easy for early socialists to recognize these civil liberties as a prerequisite for such public self-legislation, had they only thought to apply their own concept of social freedom to this new form of political action. In this case they could have viewed the right to individual liberty as a first step toward free participation in the collective activity of discussion and decision making, which obviously exhibits the same pattern of mutual supplementation as the common satisfaction of needs in the economy. Had they thus expanded the idea of social freedom, they would have understood that democratic will-formation is a communicative act whose free exercise requires that all participants possess the basic right of freedom of opinion. But it was impossible to incorporate basic liberal rights into socialist thinking, because the latter did not accord any independent role to democratic politics. Instead, most socialists believed that the cooperative regulation of their labor activities would obviate any future need for public legislation.

Finally, this astounding blindness to the democratic significance of basic rights also explains why socialists were long incapable of allying with radical liberal republicans.[9] After all, the latter also emerged from the attempt to realize the still unredeemed promises of the French Revolution by reinterpreting its guiding principles. The only difference is that liberal republicans did not base their reinterpretation on the flaws of the economic sphere, but on the deficits of the new state institutions. They saw the crucial flaw in these institutions in their failure to take sufficient account of the popular will in the legislative process. Their postrevolutionary reform efforts thus consisted in the struggle for the equal participation of all citizens in the legislative process, all in the name of egalitarianism. Even a cursory look at their list of demands reveals that they also call – at a different place and with a different emphasis – for interpreting the already institutionalized freedom as free and egalitarian cooperation. This would give the principle of popular sovereignty the necessary character of a democratic deliberative procedure. Even if German Republicans such as Julius Fröbel or radical French democrats such as Léon Gambetta never used the expression, their works plainly show that they sought to make the idea of social freedom fruitful for democratic politics.[10] The disadvantages of early socialists' inability to accept the functional differentiation of modern societies as a normative fact can also be seen in an entirely different place. Like the political sphere of action, the private sphere, i.e. the social domain of marriage and family, could also have been regarded as a field for the realization of social freedom, even though this idea was originally intended to apply solely to the economy. Contrary to their view of civil rights, which they in no way attempted to reform or expand, but to abolish altogether, nearly all of the first-generation socialists saw an intense need to overcome the traditional family model in which women were subordinated to and dependent upon men. Proudhon is an unfortunate exception, since he sought throughout his life to preserve the patriarchal family and accorded the role of raising children and housework exclusively to women.[11] Soon after, the Saint-Simonists would set out to find institutional solutions to male dominance in marriage and family life,[12] and 50 years later Friedrich Engels would publish his famous investigation of the "Origins of the Family", tracing male dominance in this sphere back to the commanding power of private property.[13] But none of the socialist authors who took up the cause of the women's movement in the nineteenth century even dreamed of employing the same model they used for conceiving of revolutionary relations of production in order to determine the conditions of freedom and equality in the sphere of personal relationships. Even though they obviously based their whole concept of social freedom in the economic sphere on the model of love, early socialists made no effort to apply this concept to the project of emancipating women from the constraints of marriage and the family. This, however, would have been the right path, for all relationships of love and affection since the beginning of modernity can be understood as relations founded on the normative idea that those involved mutually supplement and enable each other to realize themselves. In this sphere, therefore, it is clear that the freedom of each is the condition for the freedom of the other.[14] So it should have been easy for the socialists to take their own idea of social freedom – adapted to the special case of love – as a template for marriage and the family, so that family members could freely supplement each other in their life plans. The fact that they did not do so, thus missing the chance to make their original vision of social freedom more fruitful, must be traced back to their total inability to recognize the functional differentiation of modern societies. Whenever they make any claims about the future shape of the family, they do so solely in terms of the relations of production, i.e. solely in terms of the role of the family in labor relations, rather than in an independent sphere in which particular forms of social freedom should be realized.[15]

Clearly, this is the same mistake that underlies socialists' inability to make productive use of liberal rights to freedom: Because they did not recognize the independent moral logic of private relationships and were convinced that they could resort to a kind of economic monism, they saw no reason to develop an independent semantics of freedom for the sphere of love, marriage and the family. The only thing that early socialists could offer in terms of solidarity with the emerging women's movement was formulated in economic categories, and correspondingly amounted to emancipating women from male domination by integrating them into associative relations of production.[16] For decades, despite a number of attempts at mutual rapprochement, the relationship between the socialist worker's movement and the emerging feminist movement remained tense and unhappy. Although it became increasingly clear that women's liberation not only required greater equality in terms of voting and labor rights, but also a fundamental cultural change beginning with established forms of socialization if women's voices were to be freed from the gender stereotypes imposed upon them, the worker's movement remained blind to such conclusions, clinging instead to the priority of the economic sphere.[17] How different the relationship between socialism and feminism could have been had socialists only been willing to take account of the functional differentiation of modern societies by interpreting the sphere of personal relationships as an independent field of social freedom. Had they done so, the moral standard of free cooperation in social attachments based on mutual love soon would have opened their eyes to the fact that the oppression of women begins within the family, where stereotypes are imposed upon them with open or subtle forms of violence, leaving them no chance to explore their own sentiments, desires and interests. The problem, therefore, did not so much consist in involving women equally in economic production, but in granting them authorship over their own self-image, independent of male ascriptions. The struggle for social freedom in the sphere of love, marriage and the family would have primarily meant enabling women to attain as much freedom as possible from economic dependency, violence-based tutelage and one-sided labor within the hatchery of male power. This would enable women to become equal partners in relationships based on mutuality, and it is only on the basis of free and reciprocal affection that both sides would have been capable of emotionally supporting each other and articulating the needs and desires they view as a true expression of their selves.

But the early socialists chose not to employ the concept of social freedom when it came to personal relationships and develop an independent criterion for improving the situation of women. They thus proved blind not only to the rational contents of republican aims, but also to the objection that achieving gender equality would primarily entail creating the necessary prerequisites for the free articulation of genuinely feminine experiences. A century later, this demand would go by the name of "difference".[18] The inability to recognize the normative significance of these two movements once again reveals just how narrow the socio-theoretical horizon of socialism had always been. Incapable of recognizing the point of struggles to realize social freedoms in other, non-economic spheres, they were only capable of either ignoring "left" republicanism and radical feminism or accusing them of "bourgeois" class betrayal as soon as the latter's aims could not be integrated into socialism's own, exclusively economic aims. And once over the course of the twentieth century both of these two movements had become too powerful to be ignored, socialists sought to get a grip on the complex situation by introducing the unfortunate distinction between "principal and secondary contradictions". This merely revealed just how strongly socialists sought to cling to the industrialist tradition of economic determinism.[19] The attempt to renew socialism by correcting its lacking awareness of functional differentiation is, however, a much more difficult undertaking than might appear at first sight. It is not enough to merely replace the "economocentrism" of socialism with the notion of independent spheres of action which obey independent norms. Rather, a politically motivating, future-oriented project also requires an idea of how these normatively differentiated spheres should be related to each other in the future.

Before we can directly address this question, we should first review the results of our inquiry into the inability of classical socialism to differentiate between different social spheres. We began with the observation that none of the early socialists made any effort to make the idea of social freedom fruitful for other fields of social reproduction beside the economy. Instead, they were content to analyze the capitalist economy and develop measures to bring about a stronger association between the members of society. They did so without even considering whether other spheres crucial to social reproduction should also be viewed in terms of the realization of social freedom. As we have seen, none of the early socialists were willing to recognize the gradual functional differentiation of modern societies. Trapped entirely within the spirit of industrialism, and thus convinced that a future socialist society would be determined exclusively by the sphere of industrial production, they saw no reason to consider the existent or desirable independence of social spheres of action. This refusal to even consider a process of functional differentiation also explains why socialists made no effort to apply the idea of social freedom to other spheres of action. If such subsystems cannot possibly have their own independent logic, since everything is determined by economic principles and orientations, then it is not necessary to search for independent forms of realizing social freedom.[20] If we wish to take back this false step in socialist theory, then we need to argue for our assumption that the other constitutive spheres of society also depend on specific forms of social freedom. Furthermore, if socialism is still to represent the vision of a better form of life, then we must define how these independent spheres of social freedom are to relate to each other adequately in the future. I have already given an indication of the solution to the first of these tasks in my critique of the failure of traditional socialism to recognize the independence of both democracy and personal relationships. If we understand the constitutive rules of these spheres as enabling individuals to view their actions as contributions to a mutually supplementary "We", then it makes sense to presume that these spheres are also based on social freedom. From this perspective, not only the economic subsystem of action, but also personal relationships and democratic will-formation can be understood as social subsystems in which the desired results only come about if the participants are able to interpret their contributions as being free and mutually compatible. For the sphere of love, marriage and the family, the realization of social freedom means realizing new forms of relationships in which the mutual care promised by these relationships is only possible if the members involved can freely articulate their actual needs and interests with the aid of the others. For the sphere of democratic politics, this means that the participants must be able to view their individual opinions as mutually complementary contributions to the shared project of general will-formation.[21] In both cases, and as is also true of the economic system, it would be wrong to adopt the liberal conception according to which social subsystems are to give subjects the opportunity to realize private, merely individually defined intentions, thus compelling us to view attachments and mutual commitments as latent threats.[22] A revised socialism, by contrast, assumes that all three spheres of action require free cooperation and thus social freedom.[23] This form of socialism cannot, therefore, content itself with abolishing heteronomy and alienated labor in the economic sphere. Instead, it must realize that modern society cannot be genuinely *social* as long as the spheres of personal relationships and democratic politics have not been freed of coercion and influence.

Although this gives us an initial impression of why a renewed socialism should differentiate its central concept and apply it to social spheres it has hitherto ignored, this does not suffice to offer a new, more complex version of the traditional socialist vision of a better form of life. This entails much more than interpreting differentiated subsystems as situations that permit a greater amount of social freedom. It also requires a concept of the adequate relation between these subsystems. If socialism does not want to abandon its traditional vision of a future way of life necessitated by the forces of history and tangible enough to awaken the willingness to realize it at least experimentally, then it must be able to say something about how the different spheres of social freedom are to harmonize with each other in the future.

At this difficult juncture, we can draw on intuitions in the work of Hegel, and also partially in the works of Marx. In his philosophy of society, Hegel obviously envisioned the structure of social spheres with differentiated functions as a kind of living organism. His description of modern society presents an orchestrated cooperation among the various subsystems, which serves to preserve society as an organic whole. Like the organs of the body, the various social spheres relate to each other by means of their independent functions, which in turn serve the overarching aim of social reproduction. The puzzling thing about the internal rationality of such a division of labor – i.e. the unspoken contributions that the independently operating segments of society make to the functioning of a superordinate whole – becomes immediately apparent once we recognize that Hegel is applying the properties of living organisms to social entities.[24] If we leave aside the question as to whether there is empirical evidence of such organic models in the past and the present – here we could raise a number of objections[25] – we can nevertheless take it as a good reason to consider the following: If a society is to be well ordered and intact, then the relationship between its various subsystems and the overarching goal of social reproduction will have to ensure this reproduction by means of the interdependence of differentiated social spheres. Marx appears to have entertained a similar idea when he locates the fault of all history in the constant reappearance of a disjunction between forces of production and relations of production.[26] Such a crisis, i.e. a constantly reappearing disjunction between two subsystems, in turn presupposes that the future, crisis-free society is described in terms of "organic" cooperation between different functions.[27]

If we understand this organic analogy in a normative sense, then it can serve us as a criterion for determining the adequate relation between the three spheres of freedom. As I have already shown, it is not enough for a renewed socialism to discover the potential for freedom in personal relationships, the economy and democratic will-formation. It must also have a rough idea about the relation of interdependence between these different spheres. If we – like Hegel and Marx – resort to the analogy of an organism in order to solve this problem, then it seems logical that the inner rationality of this whole should constitute the desired relationship between these three spheres. Their relationship should enable them to follow their own, independent norms while at the same time freely cooperating in order to ensure the continuous reproduction of the society as a whole. Such purposeful cooperation between independent spheres of freedom represents the quintessence of a democratic way of life. This conception anticipates the formal and still abstract structures of social life – which are to be concretized through experimentation – in which subjects cooperatively contribute in their personal, economic and political relationships to the task of maintaining their community. "Democracy" does not merely signify free and equal participation in political will-formation; understood as an entire way of life, it means that individuals can participate equally at every central point in the mediation between the individual and society, such that each functionally differentiated sphere reflects the general structure of democratic participation.[28]

This idea of a democratic way of life is how socialism should conceive of an emancipated society, and it has the advantage of doing justice to the independence of various functional social spheres, but without having to abandon hopes for a harmonious whole. In order to be able to speak of a *form* of life in such a functionally differentiated society, we must assume a rationally integrated, harmoniously arranged order that represents more than the mere sum of its parts. The point is to draw the dividing lines between the three spheres of social freedom in a skillful way, thus ensuring that they support each other – like the organs of the body – in free mutuality in the reproduction of the superordinate entity of society.[29] Put this way, it is obvious that this image of a better future depends entirely on applying the traditional socialist idea of social freedom to society as a whole. It is not enough for producers, nor for the citizens of the polity, nor for those involved in personal relationships to engage in relationships of mutual supplementation in order to realize shared goals; rather, this same relationship must also be established between these various spheres. No element of such a revised socialism is more Hegelian than Marxist than the transfer of social freedom to social units as a whole. The society of the future should no longer be conceived of as an order steered centrally from below, i.e. from within the relations of production, but as an organic whole of independent and yet purposefully cooperating functions in which the members act for each other in social freedom. This anticipation of future society, this idea of free cooperation between intersubjective spheres of freedom in the interest of the superordinate goal of social reproduction should not, however, be misunderstood as a fixed vision of the future which is immune to change. Just like all of the anticipatory elements of the theory, this "primary" guiding conception must be understood as giving us orientation and nothing more, as pointing out the direction our experimental search for institutional possibilities should take. The social conditions which, on the basis of experience-based knowledge, must be established in the various spheres of society in order to enable the egalitarian cooperation of its members must follow the superordinate perspective required for making appropriate distinctions. In other words, every possible change should be re-examined in terms of whether it gives each independent sphere enough space to grow eventually into an organ of democratic life, while still operating according to its own norms.

However, we still need to clarify two further issues

in order to give a revised socialism the power to effect transformational change. First, our sketch of a democratic way of life may give the fatal impression that there is no need for a steering authority capable of initiating exploratory changes and establishing a continuous research process. Our "organic" analogy suggests that we should, similar to structural functionalism, conceive of these transformational processes as the result of an anonymous, overarching purposeful activity which does not demand active investigation.[30] Therefore, we must correct our orientational schema so as to make visible the location within the interplay among the various spheres of social freedom from which to steer the necessary processes of transformation, delineation, and adaptation. Only once we have determined the appropriate reflexive authority can a renewed socialism gain clarity about what it needs to do and what it needs to influence in order to initiate experimentation on the social organism. Moreover, our future vision has not yet clearly identified the social points of reference for the idea of a democratic way of life. Generally, the answer to this question simply assumes that the nation-state represents the framework within which the required transformational processes are to take place. However, given the growing interdependence between individual states and the accompanying processes of transnationalization, this assumption has become highly implausible, forcing socialism once again to clarify its relationship to the nation-state.[31]

The first of these two gaps raises the problem of how to reconcile the notion of an organic interaction between independent spheres of freedom with the notion of an active center that can take over the necessary tasks of coordination and delineation. The answer to this question touches on the important issue as to the addressees of a revised socialism that conceives of society as a functional differentiated structure, thus placing social actors into a variety of social roles. After all, there is no longer merely an opposition between "workers" and "capitalists", but also equally relevant and conflictual antagonisms between family members and citizens of the polity. Just to give a sense of the serious difficulties involved in distinguishing between these reference groups, we might think of how simple and clear this entire complex was for classical socialism. Since the latter denied any functional differentiation, it could think of society as an entity determined entirely by the economic sphere and make the proletariat the sole addressee of its theory, since the workers' productive labor represented the central lever for steering society in the past, the present and the future. But if, for good reasons, we abandon this economic determinism and cautiously replace it with a conception of normatively independent functional spheres, then there can no longer be just the *one* actor who, by virtue of his activity in a crucial sector of social reproduction, could also oversee the future shaping of the private sphere and the political system of action. Instead, we can assume a plurality of functionally specific actors in charge of the configuration of their respective domain, which means that our socio-theoretically enlightened socialism is in danger of losing its one main addressee. Clearly, the only way out of the predicament of having to send distinct, sphere-specific messages to entirely different addressees is to find an institution or authority that could manage the relation between all these independent spheres. The subjects active in this institution could then function as the collective which socialists today could attempt to convince of their vision of a democratic way of life in order to motivate these actors to undertake experimental explorations.

At this point as well, we should turn to John Dewey, who was likely the first theorist to systematically address the issue of which social organ in a complex society is capable of reflexively steering the desired development of a complex society.[32] Under different intellectual circumstances, Emile Durkheim presented similar considerations even earlier,[33] and Jürgen Habermas took the same issue even further.[34] The solution Dewey proposed counts today as everyday pragmatic knowledge and can be understood as a continuation of the already mentioned notion that at the stage of the social, unused potentials for social renewal can only be discovered through a process of communication which is as unrestricted as possible.[35] If we take this idea further and determine which authority within a functionally arranged society should take over the task of integrative steering, it will become obvious that the appropriate institution is that of a "public sphere" in which all participants take part as freely as possible. Due to the plurality of voices and perspectives, citizens' cooperation would enable them to quickly notice problems in individual spheres and in their interaction, thus also enabling a number of proposals for modifications. Translated back into the organic terms I have used thus far, the subsystem of action best suited to the task of reflexively steering overall social reproduction is that which provides the institutional framework for democratic will-formation. The sphere of democratic action stands out among the other functionally complementary spheres of freedom; it is *prima inter pares*, because it is the only place in which problems from every corner of social life can be articulated for all ears and be presented as a task to be solved in cooperation.[36] In addition to the epistemic leading role of the political public sphere, and owing to its legitimizing influence on the legislature, this is the only social sphere with the power to turn seemingly plausible solutions into law. There can be no doubt that the democratic public sphere, occupied by deliberating citizens, must take over the role of supervising the functioning of the entire organic structure and of making the requisite adjustments. Functional differentiation, which thus far seemed to take place automatically, now becomes an object of democratic politics.[37] In the democratic way of life, that which unfolds automatically in a living organism as the result of its internal structure, i.e. the development that results from the interaction of mutually supporting and mutually dependent organs, is brought about by the subjects of the democratic process. They are the ones who correct and adjust the outcome of the entirety of their own activity by means of public deliberation.

This perspective on a consummately democratic form of life also resolves the issue of whom renewed socialism must call upon to carry on the struggle to expand our social freedoms by means of experimental explorations. The citizens assembled in the democratic public sphere are the only ones who can be convinced to tear down existing limitations and blockages cautiously in order to enable free cooperation in all major social spheres. Neither a certain social class – be it the industrial proletariat or addled white-collar workers – nor some other social movement can be considered the primary addressee of socialism. Socialists today should attempt instead to influence all those who, within the sphere of democratic interaction, have an open ear for complaints over grievances, discrimination and the use of power, all of which point to symptomatic restrictions within the various spheres of society. Social classes or movements can no longer serve as a guarantee for future success, for as we have seen,[38] the assumption that a certain social situation automatically entails the will to revolution has collapsed like a house of cards. The belief that certain collective subjectivities have a world-historical task should be replaced by the belief that the course of progress embodied by institutional achievements will not tolerate an arbitrary break and will thus continue on into the future. In this case, it is not a disadvantage, but even advantageous that socialism is now faced with a democratic public sphere, i.e. an addressee that is not a collective subjectivity at all due to the fact that its social composition is constantly in flux. It is precisely this openness, this pulsing attentiveness to the most diverse topics and perspectives which guarantee that complaints over restrictions on freedom will in fact be heard from all corners of the social structure in order to be measured against the historical narrative of a continuing line of progress. In order to view the citizens assembled in the public sphere as the addressee of socialism's messages, therefore, we must not only abandon the illusion of a fixed, already existing bearer of the socialist cause, but also seek to politically represent strivings for emancipation in all subsystems of society according to the normative guideline of "social freedom". If socialism today no longer merely seeks to abolish heteronomy and alienated labor in the economic sphere, but to overcome coercion and domination in personal relationships and democratic will-formation, then its allies will only be found in the arenas of the political public sphere. It is only here that socialism can encounter the members of society in roles that enable them to commit to improvements not directly related to their own interests. Today, therefore, socialism is primarily the cause of political citizens, not wage-workers – as much as the latter's needs are what will need to be fought for in the future.

We still need to deal with a question that reaches far back into the history of the workers' movement: Must socialism be understood as a national or as an internationalist project? The answer to this question is much more difficult than might appear at first sight, given the contemporary blurring of national borders. On the one hand, it seems obvious – at least more so than in the nineteenth century at the start of the socialist movement – that we should understand the vision of socialism as a socio-political project which can only be realized by transcending the borders of the nation-state. After all, the normative regulation of the various spheres of action today seems so strongly removed from the "sovereign" control of individual nation-states that it seems almost impossible to realize all the desired improvements in these spheres within a single country. Here we need only think of the capitalist economic system, which has long become far too international for it to be controlled sufficiently by individual nation-states. The socialist doctrine must therefore progress along with this tendency toward international interdependence by no longer respecting national borders in its experimental search for possibilities of expanding social freedom.

And because, as we have seen, the initiative for such experimental explorations must somehow come from the democratic public sphere, this initiative would soon need to be transnationalized in order to be able to stand up to opposing international forces. But this is all easier said than done.[39] Furthermore, this cannot do justice to a social reality which always poses more imbalances and disjunctures than the term "global society" might suggest.[40]

The difficulties begin once we realize that the previously differentiated spheres of action are affected to much different degrees by the tendency toward global regulation. Although the economic system is largely controlled by "global society", this is in no way true for the family or for intimate relationships and friendships, which are still largely determined by the moral and legal conditions prevailing in individual countries or cross-country cultures. Whereas gay marriage is becoming more and more legitimate and legal in Europe, it remains unthinkable in other regions due to prevalent traditions. Furthermore, the functionally differentiated social order largely relies on guarantees provided by constitutions and basic rights intended to enable the members of society to shift freely between different roles. As long as constitutional regulations are created and guaranteed by individual sovereign states, it would surely be unwise to refrain entirely from national processes of social differentiation.[41] Ulrich's Beck demand that the "methodology" of social theory must henceforth be strictly cosmopolitan[42] is far too hasty, because it fails to take into account the degree to which major segments of social reality continue to be determined by national systems of rules. A third difficulty facing the attempt to renew socialism is the temporal gap between the fact of growing internationalization and social consciousness. Even if the normative rules of individual spheres of action are increasingly determined at a transnational level, a significant part of the population still assumes that "their" nation-state institutions are able to legislate and re-legislate democratically. We would misunderstand this lag of public opinion if we merely put it down to a lacking sense of reality or to the idolatry of everyday consciousness. Instead, we should presume it to be an expression of the political-practical need to ascribe consequential events in our surroundings to generally visible authorities that can be held to account or called upon to intervene. Whatever the appropriate interpretation of this disjuncture, of this gap between real developments and their public perception, it represents a difficult challenge for the attempt to revive socialism. After all, we cannot merely skip over the "lagging" consciousness of citizens, because we have to win them over for our project. On the other hand, however, the true extent of the state's loss of sovereignty cannot be denied just for the sake of gaining public consent as quickly as possible. Whereas in the first case this would give rise to the danger of avant-gardism or elitism, here it would give rise to the danger of populism.

All these disjunctures only make clear how hasty and imprudent it would be to claim that socialism is an obviously and solely "internationalist" project. Certainly, socialism does aim to foster experimental explorations across the globe that seek to bring about a democratic form of life. It seeks to guide attempts in all countries to foster free and equal cooperation in the spheres of personal relationships, economic activity and political will-formation, which together would form an organic form of life. In this normative sense, socialism is a "cosmopolitan" or "internationalist" undertaking – what else? It not only calls upon the citizens of Europe or other economically developed regions, but on all citizens worldwide, to go beyond the liberal interpretation of the principles of the French Revolution and realize freedom, equality and fraternity in a way that makes society more "social". If this vision is to bring together experiments on expanding our social freedoms in the most diverse places, then socialism must also represent more than a merely moral variety of internationalism. It must act as a worldwide movement in which local projects supplement each other by supporting all kinds of socio-political efforts wherever they may be underway. To insert all in a single formula, in this kind of socialist internationalism, experimental interventions in one place should improve the prospects for experiments elsewhere. And if these interdependencies prove so strong that interventions can only be successfully tested worldwide – e.g. Thomas Piketty's global tax for the purpose of sustainable redistribution[43] – then such interventions must fulfill the demanding condition that they simultaneously reach political decision makers in all states. However, both cases – mutual supplementation and a global network of local experiments – are predicated on the existence of a global organizational center on the model of Amnesty International or Greenpeace, with chapters in as many countries as possible that can take over the necessary work of coordination. Therefore, if socialism is to live up to the new international order, it will have to follow the model of globally successful non-governmental organizations and become an international representative organ for the moral aim of realizing social freedoms.

Beneath the level of a transnational organization, however, socialism must remain rooted in geographical spaces with enough cultural and legal commonalities to enable public spheres to come about at all. If socialists' demands are primarily addressed to those who actively and publicly work to remove social ills, this presupposes that moral sensibilities and foci converge enough to permit common action on the basis of shared diagnoses. Therefore, it is secondary whether these public spaces are limited to individual nations or already bear international features. More important is that the potential addressees' moral sensibilities overlap enough to enable them to grasp the realization of social freedoms as a common challenge. Given the existence of global interdependencies, it makes sense to articulate the need for socialism and organize the socialist project on a global scale; for the purposes of mobilizing citizens for political action, however, socialism must take local action wherever possibilities for collective action are clearly visible. At this level, socialism must convince its addressees of the need to uncover potentials for stronger cooperation concealed in the existing social order, thus uncovering the possibilities for realizing social freedom in the future.

This tension between internationalism and an anchoring in local traditions means that socialism must appear in two shapes at once. Drawing on a famous distinction made by John Rawls,[44] we could perhaps say that socialism can only represent social freedom globally by means of a political doctrine, whereas it can only mobilize concrete and local publics by means of an ethically compact theory adapted to the cultural features of a certain region. In its first role as an intellectual link between various international struggles, it must abstract from individual ethical forms in order to emphasize their compatibility with the principles of social freedom. Yet in its second role as a source of ideas for local social experimentation, socialism must be transformed back into a culturally saturated and comprehensive "global theory" (Rawls) in order to win not just the minds, but also the hearts of those involved. When it comes to the "global public", we could say that socialism can only be a "political", ethically neutralized doctrine. In relation to its respective addressees, it can only take the shape of a theory that generates meaning for a certain life-world.[45]

Yet this balancing act between two different shapes of one and the same idea should not pose too great a difficulty, as long as socialists focus their efforts on cracking open certain life-world forms of ethical life [*Sittlichkeiten*] and making them morally sensitive to external affairs. No local public sphere is so impenetrable as to be incapable of registering the needs and desires of others in the world. Therefore, when it comes to formulating common challenges, all of these public spheres must take account of these external demands when dealing with local challenges. All collective addressees of the socialist project are so caught in the pull of moral transnationalization that they can no longer ignore the demands of other addressees. This is the present developmental tendency socialists must rely upon if they are to reduce the gap between socialism's two different theoretical branches. When it comes to winning over different public spheres for the project of experimentally expanding social freedoms, it must stand up clearly for all excluded groups in order to take account of their interests in the overall search for adequate solutions. The more successful we are in integrating others into our own local efforts to expand the scope of social freedom, the smaller the gap between the two shapes of socialist theory will turn out to be. With each additional, "external" voice we integrate into local experimental processes, the circle of those who count as members of the experimental public sphere, and thus as addressees of an ethically charged and comprehensive doctrine, will expand. Whether we can ultimately close the gap between both varieties of socialism by cracking open local public spheres remains to be seen. Only experiments guided by the idea of social freedom can offer the answers that will gradually enable us to get a sense of the future in order to then cautiously appropriate it.

***

These far-reaching reflections bring me to the end of my attempt to free socialism from the shackles of nineteenth-century thought and give it a form that is more appropriate to the present. I have needed to take a number of detours and draw on the ideas of other intellectual traditions in order to lay the theoretical groundwork for the project of harmonizing liberty, equality and solidarity in a way that overcomes liberalism from within. This has required abandoning once and for all the idea that the proletariat represents a revolutionary subject, replacing the socialist pioneers' conception of history with a kind of historical experimentalism and adapting the idea of social freedom to the circumstances of social differentiation. But above all, this has demanded replacing the vision of an economically administered society with the vision of a democratic way of life. This has meant recasting socialism in a way that would make its main purpose and theoretical impulse unrecognizable to the majority of its previous followers. There no longer seems to be any hope that capitalism will eventually bring about its own demise, nor that the working class bears within itself the seed of the new society. Yet, those who see this as a reason to cast doubt on my proposal of a revised socialism will have to ask themselves whether their insistence on clinging to their illusions will in fact cause them to miss what is perhaps their last chance to restore some hope in the realizability of their own project. How much more realistic would it be today to base our hopes for the transformability of the given social order not on the power of an individual class, but on the traces of social progress in whose realization socialism has played such a decisive role for 200 years. How much more appropriate to today's changed consciousness of conflict would it be if socialists became advocates of the expansion of freedom not merely in the relations of production but also in personal relationships and political opportunities for co-determination?

Once we apply the notion of social freedom to all three constitutive spheres of modern societies (not just the economy, but also politics and personal relationships), we will finally see the full extent of what the original socialist vision should stand for today. Within liberal-democratic capitalism, it represents the historical tendency to gradually overcome social dependency and exclusion by constantly pointing out that the realization of the promised harmony between freedom, equality and solidarity is not possible under the prevailing social conditions. This would first require transforming all major spheres of action that represent the institutional prerequisites for free cooperation. Socialists cannot content themselves with the prospect of removing heteronomy and alienated labor in the economic sphere, because they know that modern society cannot be genuinely social as long as coercion and domination continue to exist in the spheres of personal relationships and democratic politics. Compared to the theoretical self-understanding of the first generation of socialists, this fundamentally renewed socialism can be both more and less. On the one hand, it cannot restrict its visions of a better future to the economic project of collectivizing the sphere of economic activity, because it has learned that the conditions of social freedom must also be realized in the family and intimate relationships, as well as in procedures of public will-formation. On the other hand, it can no longer rely on the knowledge of historical necessities. It must instead discover the need for change in these spheres by means of experimental exploration and the acquisition of new knowledge.

Despite the need to constantly adapt its ends and means, the aim of a revised socialism, i.e. what its encouraging look back at the historical symbols, found in reforms that have already been achieved, should point to in the future, must be a social form of life in which individual freedom thrives not at the cost of solidarity, but with its help. Ultimately I can think of no better image of this aim than that of the free interplay of all social freedoms in the difference of their respective functions. Only if all members of society can satisfy the needs they share with all others – physical and emotional intimacy, economic independence and political self-determination – by relying on the sympathy and support of their partners in interaction will our society have become social in the full sense of the term.

Notes

Preface

1 Axel Honneth, *Freedom's Right: The Social Foundations of Democratic Life* (Cambridge: Polity, 2014).

2 See the various contributions in the Special Issue on Axel Honneth's Freedom's Right, *Critical Horizons*, vol. 16, no. 2 (2015).

3 Axel Honneth, "Rejoinder", ibid., pp. 204–26.

Introduction

1 Samuel Moyn, *The Last Utopia: Human Rights in History* (Cambridge, MA: Harvard University Press, 2010).

2 Titus Stahl, *Immanente Kritik: Elemente einer Theorie sozialer Praktiken* (Frankfurt/Main: Campus, 2013).

3 Karl Marx, *Capital, Volume I* (London: Penguin, 1990), p. 165.

4 See Jacques Rancière, *Proletarian Nights: The Workers' Dream in Nineteenth-Century France* (London: Verso, 2012).

5 See Pierre Bourdieu et al., *The Weight of the World: Social Suffering in Contemporary Society* (Stanford, CA: Stanford University Press, 1999).

6 Barrington Moore, *Injustice: The Social Bases of Obedience and Revolt* (New York: Random House, 1979), esp. ch. 14.

I. The Original Idea: The Consummation of the Revolution in Social Freedom

1 Wolfgang Schieder, "Sozialismus", in O. Brunner, W. Conze, and R. Koselleck, eds, *Geschichtliche Grundbegriffe: Historisches Lexikon zur politisch-sozialen Sprache in Deutschland, Vol. 5* (Stuttgart: Klett-Cotta, 1984), pp. 923–96, here: pp. 924–7.

2 Ibid., pp. 930–4.

3 Ibid., pp. 934–9. Carl Grünberg traces this new usage of the term "socialist" to the followers of Robert Owen in England in the 1820s: "Der Ursprung der Worte 'Sozialismus' und 'Sozialist'", *Archiv für die Geschichte des Sozialismus und der Arbeiterbewegung*, Vol. 2 (1912), pp. 372–9.

4 Hans Heinz Holz, "Einleitung", in H.H. Holz, ed., G.W. Leibniz, *Politische Schriften II* (Frankfurt/Main: Europäische Verlagsanstalt, 1967), pp. 5–20.

5 Gottfried Wilhelm Leibniz, "Sozietät und Wirtschaft" [1671], in *Politische Schriften II*, pp. 127–30, here: p. 129.

6 Charles Fourier, *The Theory of the Four Movements* (Cambridge: Cambridge University Press, 1996), p. xviii.

7 It was only after Owen had visited Fourier in Paris in 1937 that they both decided to present themselves as being "socialists". See Schieder, "Socialism", p. 936.

8 On the origin and history of socialism, see George Lichtheim, *Ursprünge des Sozialismus* (Gütersloh: Bertelsmann, 1969); *Kurze Geschichte des Sozialismus* (Frankfurt/Main, Vienna and Zurich: Kiepenhauer & Witsch, 1977); G.D.H. Cole, *Socialist Thought, Vol. 1: The Forerunners 1789–1850* (London: Macmillan & Co., 1955); Jacques Droz, ed., *Histoire générale de socialisme, Vol. 2, 1875–1918* (Paris: PUF, 1997). An interesting analysis in the sociology of knowledge is provided by Robert Wuthnow, *Communities of Discourse: Ideology and Social Structure in the Reformation, the Enlightenment, and European Socialism* (Cambridge, MA: Harvard University Press, 1989), part III.

9 Emile Durkheim, *Socialism and Saint Simon* (London: Routledge, 1959), p. 19: "We denote as socialist every doctrine which demands the connection of all economic functions, or of certain of them, which are at the present time diffuse, to the directing and conscious centers of society." John Dewey provides a very similar definition in his *Lectures in China, 1919–1920* (Honolulu, HI: University of Hawai'i Press, 1973), pp. 117ff.

10 On this connection to the ideals of the French Revolution, see Wuthnow, *Communities of Discourse*, pp. 370ff.

11 John Stuart Mill, "Chapters on Socialism", in *Principles of Political Economy* (Oxford: Oxford Paperbacks, 1998), pp. 369–436; Joseph Schumpeter, "Sozialistische Möglichkeiten von heute", in *Aufsätze zur ökonomischen Theorie* (Tübingen: Mohr, 1952), pp. 465–510.

12 Robert Owen, "A New View of Society" [1813–

1816], in *A New View of Society and Other Writings* (London: Penguin Classics, 1991), pp. 10ff.; on Owen, see also Cole, *Socialist Thought, Vol. 1*, chs IX and XI; Droz, ed., *Geschichte des Sozialismus, Vol. II*, pp. 29–48.

13 Gottfried Salomon-Delatour, ed., *Die Lehre Saint-Simons* (Neuwied: Luchterhand, 1962); Droz, ed., *Geschichte des Sozialismus, vol. II*, pp. 113–30.

14 Fourier, *The Theory of the Four Movements*, p. xviii; Droz, ed., *Geschichte des Sozialismus, Vol. II*, pp. 131–43.

15 See Cole, *Socialist Thought, Vol. I*, ch. XIX.

16 Louis Blanc, *L'organisation du travail* (Paris: Nouveau Monde, 1850), p. 27.

17 On these differentiations, see Cole, *Socialist Thought, Vol. I*, chs XV and XIX.

18 The distinction I hereby make between two views of "socialism" is similar to the one made by David Miller, who distinguishes between two different socialist critiques of capitalism, one of which appeals to principles of distributive justice, the other of which to a certain "quality of life." David Miller, "In What Sense Must Socialism Be Communitarian?", *Social Philosophy and Policy*, vol. 6, no. 2 (1989), pp. 51–73.

19 Pierre-Joseph Proudhon, *Les confessions d'un révolutionnaire* (Paris: Garnier Frères, 1851), p. 233.

20 Ibid.

21 See especially Proudhon's considerations on the principle of "mutuality", ibid., p. 242.

22 In the following I will only discuss the works of Marx to the extent that it is relevant to the self-

understanding of the socialist movement. In no way do I intend to undertake a fundamental discussion of his theory as a whole. Much could be said about this on various points.

23 Karl Marx, "Excerpts from James Mill's Elements of Political Economy" [1844], in *Karl Marx: Early Writings* (London: Penguin, 1992), pp. 259–78; see also, among others, Daniel Brudney, "The Young Marx and the Middle-Aged Rawls", in J. Mandle and D. Reidy, eds, *A Companion to Rawls* (London: Wiley-Blackwell, 2014), pp. 450–71; see on the entire topic: David Archard, "The Marxist Ethic of Self-Realization: Individuality and Community", *Royal Institute of Philosophy Lecture Series*, vol. 22 (1987), pp. 19–34.

24 Marx, "Excerpts from James Mill's Elements of Political Economy", p. 266.

25 Ibid., p. 275

26 Ibid., p. 275–6.

27 Ibid, p. 277.

28 See the interpretation of this passage offered by Brudney, "Der junge Marx und der mittlere Rawls", pp. 127–33.

29 Marx, "Excerpts from James Mill's Elements of Political Economy", p. 277.

30 Brudney, "The Young Marx and the Middle-Aged Rawls", p. 454.

31 On this decisive step, see Jerome B. Schneewind, *The Invention of Autonomy* (Cambridge: Cambridge University Press, 1998), chs 22 and 23.

32 Isaiah Berlin, "Two Concepts of Liberty," in *Liberty* (Oxford: Oxford University Press, 2002), pp. 166–217.

33 On Rousseau, see Frederick Neuhouser, *Rousseau's Theodicy of Self-Love: Evil, Rationality, and the Drive for Recognition* (Oxford: Oxford University Press, 2008), esp. pp. 76, 122, 148–51; on Marx, see Lawrence A. Hamilton, *The Political Philosophy of Needs* (Cambridge: Cambridge University Press, 2003), pp. 53–62.

34 Friedrich August von Hayek, *The Constitution of Liberty* (Chicago, IL: University of Chicago Press, 1960).

35 Quentin Skinner, *Liberty Before Liberalism* (Cambridge: Cambridge University Press, 1998); Philip Pettit, *Just Freedom: A Moral Compass for a Complex World* (New York: Norton, 2014).

36 On Hegel's concept of freedom, see Axel Honneth, "Von der Armut unserer Freiheit: Größe und Grenzen der hegelschen Sittlichkeitslehre", in A. Honneth & G. Hindrichs, eds, *Freiheit: Internationaler Hegelkongress 2011* (Frankfurt/Main: Klostermann, 2013), pp. 13–30.

37 On this differentiation, see the excellent study by Andrew Mason, *Community, Solidarity and Belonging: Levels of Community and their Normative Significance* (Cambridge: Cambridge University Press, 2000), esp. ch. I.1, pp. 17–41.

38 Joseph Raz, *The Morality of Freedom* (Oxford: Oxford University Press, 1986), pp. 307–11; see also Mason, *Community, Solidarity and Belonging*, pp. 55f.

39 On this kind of holistic individualism, see Philip Pettit, *The Common Mind: An Essay on Psychology, Society, and Politics* (Oxford: Oxford University Press, 1993), pp. 271ff.

40 It might seem surprising at first glance that "fraternity" or "solidarity" should also belong to the principles of legitimation established in our modern democratic societies. But we can easily get a sense of this fact if we consider the idea of distributional justice, deeply anchored in democratic culture and demanding redistribution in favor of those who are worse off, thus appealing to a feeling of solidarity among all members of society. See John Rawls, *A Theory of Justice* (Oxford: Oxford University Press, 1999), pp. 90ff.

II. An Antiquated Intellectual Structure: The Spirit and Culture of Industrialism

1 See again Miller, "In What Sense Must Socialism Be Communitarian?".

2 Pettit, *The Common Mind*, pp. 271ff.

3 Benedict Anderson, *Imagined Communities: Reflections on the Origin and Spread of Nationalism* (London: Verso, 1991); see also Mason, *Community, Solidarity and Belonging*, pp. 38–40.

4 Rawls, *A Theory of Justice*, pp. 90ff.

5 The term "Western Marxism" was coined by Maurice Merleau-Ponty in *Adventures of the Dialectic* (Evanston, IL: Northwestern University Press, 1973). Ever since, it has been projected onto a very heterogeneous tradition – spanning from Lukács to Marcuse – of unorthodox, critical Marxism. For an overview, see Martin Jay, *Marxism and Totality: The Adventures of a Concept from Lukács to Habermas* (Berkeley, CA: University of California Press, 1984). For a Trotskyist and thus negative view, see the summary offered by Perry

Anderson, *Considerations on Western Marxism* (London: Verso, 1976).

6 For an initial overview, see Eduard Heimann, *Geschichte der volkswirtschaftlichen Lehrmeinungen* (Frankfurt/Main: Klostermann, 1949), ch. V.3.

7 Salomon-Delatour, ed., *Die Lehre Saint-Simons*, esp. pp. 112–30; see also the overview offered by Cole, *Socialist Thought*, chs IV and V; Droz, ed., *Geschichte des Sozialismus, Vol. II*, pp. 113–30.

8 See Pierre-Joseph Proudhon, *Théorie de la propriété* (Paris: Lacroix, Verboeckhoven et Cie, 1871); on Proudhon's "anarchism", see Jacques Droz, ed., *Geschichte des Sozialismus, Vol. III: Sozialismus und Arbeiterbewegung bis zum Ende der I. Internationale* (Frankfurt/Main: Ullstein, 1975), pp. 82–7.

9 Karl Marx, "On the Jewish Question", in *Karl Marx: Early Writings*, pp. 211–41.

10 Ibid., p. 221.

11 Ibid., p. 219.

12 From among the diverse literature on Marx's argument, here are only two contributions: Frederick Neuhouser, "Marx (und Hegel) zur Philosophie der Freiheit", in Jaeggi & Loick, eds, *Nach Marx*, pp. 25–47; Catherine Colliot-Thélène, *La démocratie sans démos* (Paris: PUF, 2011), pp. 45–54.

13 See Schieder, "Sozialismus", pp. 990ff; on the history of the party name "social democracy", see ibid., pp. 977f. On the history of German social democracy, see Detlef Lehnert, *Sozialdemokratie zwischen Protestbewegung und Regierungspartei 1848–1983* (Frankfurt/Main: Suhrkamp, 1983).

14 Eduard Bernstein offers an entirely different argument here, being the only intellectual in the

workers' movement to think through the theoretical weaknesses of industrialist socialism already at the beginning of the twentieth century. For him, democracy represents the moral core of all socialist aims, because it represents not only a political form of government based on the majority principle, but also the adequate form of organizing social life as a whole. Bernstein thus speaks quite presciently of "democracy" as the "organization of freedom". Eduard Bernstein, "Der sozialistische Begriff der Demokratie", in *Sozialdemokratische Völkerpolitik: Gesammelte Aufsätze* (Leipzig: Verlag Naturwissenschaften, 1917), pp. 1–15, here: p. 11. The radicalism of Bernstein's "revisionism" is often overlooked in the secondary literature on his work, because it is often written from a Marxist or Party perspective. Bo Gustafsson is an exception, primarily emphasizing the influence of the English Fabians: *Marxismus und Revisionismus: Eduard Bernsteins Kritik des Marxismus und ihre ideengeschichtlichen Voraussetzungen*, 2 vols (Frankfurt/Main: Europäische Verlagsanstalt, 1972), pp. 316–26.

15 See Neuhouser, "Marx (und Hegel) zur Philosophie der Freiheit".

16 See Axel Honneth, *Freedom's Right*, ch. C.III.3.

17 See Salomon-Delatour, ed., *Die Lehre Saint-Simons*, pp. 103–11; see also Droz, ed., *Geschichte des Sozialismus*, pp. 117–21.

18 The assumption of such a shared interest among all workers can be clearly seen in Louis Blanc, *L'organisation du travail*, p. 71; Proudhon also speaks in the same sense of the "destiny" of all

workers; see, for instance, his *Théorie de la propriété*, p. 104.

19 On this problem, see Cornelius Castoriadis, *The Imaginary Institution of Society* (Cambridge, MA: MIT Press, 1998), Part I; Jean L. Cohen, *Class and Civil Society: The Limits of Marxian Critical Theory* (Amherst, MA: University of Massachusetts Press, 1982). On the tension between Marx's systematic and historical writings, see Axel Honneth, "Die Moral im 'Kapital': Versuch einer Korrektur der Marxschen Ökonomiekritik", in Jaeggi & Loick, eds, *Nach Marx*, pp. 350–63.

20 See Karl Marx, *Economic and Philosophical Manuscripts of 1844* (Mineola, NY: Dover, 2007), pp. 124f.

21 See Marx's well-known formulations in *Capital*, Vol. 1, pp. 929f.

22 Institute für Sozialforschung, ed., *Studien über Autorität und Familie* [Studies on Authority and the Family] (Paris: Librairie Felix Alcan, 1936); Erich Fromm, *Arbeiter und Angestellte am Vorabend des Dritten Reiches: eine sozialpsychologische Untersuchung*, revised and with an introduction by Wolfgang Bonss (Stuttgart: Deutsche Verlagsanstalt, 1980).

23 See Daniel Bell, *The Coming of Post-Industrial Society: A Venture in Social Forecasting* (New York: Basic Books, 1973).

24 See Josef Mooser, *Arbeiterleben in Deutschland 1900–1970* (Frankfurt/Main: Suhrkamp, 1984), pp. 184f.

25 An awareness of this fact within radical socialism can most clearly be seen in the French postwar

movement "Socialisme ou Barbarie". See Cornelius Castoriadis, "Socialism or Barbarism", in D.A. Curtis, ed., *Cornelius Castoriadis: Political and Social Writings, Vol. I, 1946–1955* (Minneapolis, MN: University of Minnesota Press, 1988); on this group, see François Dosse, *Castoriadis: Une Vie* (Paris: La Découverte, 2014), chs 3 and 4. See the influential study by André Gorz, *Abschied vom Proletariat: Jenseits des Sozialismus* (Reinbek bei Hamburg: Rowohlt, 1984). In the radical left thought of post-operaism, we find a reflection of the awareness of the decline of the workers' movement in the replacement of the industrial proletariat by the "multitude" as an addressee of socialist theory: Michael Hardt & Antonio Negri, *Empire* (Cambridge, MA: Harvard University Press, 2000). The process of coping with the disappearance of what was once thought to be the "revolutionary" class takes place for the most part in literature, film and music. See Alan Sillitoe, *The Loneliness of the Long Distance Runner* (1959); Bob Dylan, Workingman's Blues #2, 2006 ("Modern Times"). An impressively sociological account of the dissolution of the classical proletariat can be found in Jefferson Cowie, *Stayin' Alive: The 1970s and the Last Days of the Working Class* (New York: The New Press, 2010).

26 See, e.g., Gerald A. Cohen, *Self-Ownership, Freedom and Equality* (Cambridge: Cambridge University Press, 1995).

27 On this tradition in the philosophy of history, to which many representatives of early socialism adhere, see Robert Nisbet, *History of the Idea of*

Progress (New York: Transaction, 1980), part II, ch. 6.

28 See Salomon-Delatour, ed., *Die Lehre Saint-Simons*, pp. 55–66; see also Cole, *Socialist Thought*, chs IV and V.

29 Salomon-Delatour, ed., *Die Lehre Saint-Simons*, pp. 125–30.

30 Cole, *Socialist Thought*, p. 169.

31 Ibid., p. 208.

32 Karl Marx, *The Poverty of Philosophy* (Moscow: Progress Publishers, 1955).

33 On this tension, see Castoriadis, *The Imaginary Institution of Society*, ch. 1.

34 Karl Marx & Friedrich Engels, *The Communist Manifesto* (London: Penguin Classics, 2002).

35 Here is only one of the many formulations Marx employs to describe this "law": *Capital*, Vol. *I*, p. 929.

36 Gerald A. Cohen, *Karl Marx's Theory of History: A Defence* (Princeton, NJ: Princeton University Press, 1978).

37 See Theodor W. Adorno, "The Idea of Natural History", *Telos*, no. 60 (1984), pp. 111–24; Alfred Schmidt, *The Concept of Nature in Marx* (London: Verso, 2014), esp. ch. III.

38 See, e.g., Dieter Groh, *Negative Integration und revolutionärer Attentismus: Die deutsche Sozialdemokratie am Vorabend des Ersten Weltkriegs* (Frankfurt/Main: Ullstein, 1974).

39 See, e.g., the debates documented in the following publications: Hans-Jörg Sandkühler, ed., *Marxismus und Ethik: Texte zum neukantianischen Sozialismus* (Frankfurt/Main: Suhrkamp, 1974); Nikolai

Bucharin & Abram Deborin, *Kontroversen über dialektischen und mechanistischen Materialismus* (Frankfurt/Main: Suhrkamp, 1974).

40 See John Dewey, *Liberalism and Social Action*, in *The Later Works, Vol. II* (1935–1937) (Carbondale, IL: Southern Illinois University Press, 1980), pp. 1–65; Maurice Merleau-Ponty presents a similar consideration against orthodox Marxism in *Adventures of the Dialectic*, pp. 52ff.

41 See, e.g., Nisbet, *History of the Idea of Progress*, Part II, ch. 6 (New York: W.W. Norton, 1996), ch. II.

III. Paths of Renewal (1): Socialism as Historical Experimentalism

1 Castoriadis, "Socialism or Barbarism"; The revisions proposed by the Yugoslavian group "Praxis" should also be mentioned in this context, e.g. Predrag Vranicki, *Marxismus und Sozialismus* (Frankfurt/Main: Suhrkamp, 1985); Gajo Petrovic, *Wider den autoritären Marxismus* (Frankfurt/Main: Europäische Verlagsanstalt, 1969).

2 Jürgen Habermas, "What Does Socialism Mean Today?", in R. Blackburn, ed., *After the Fall: The Failure of Communism and the Future of Socialism* (New York: Verso, 1991), pp. 25–46.

3 See John Roemer, ed., *Analytical Marxism* (Cambridge: Cambridge University Press, 1986); G.A. Cohen, *Self-Ownership, Freedom, and Equality* (Cambridge: Cambridge University Press, 1995). A very convincing account of the practical and political deficit of analytical Marxism can be found in Joshua Cohen and Joel Rogers, "My Utopia or

Yours", in E.O. Wright, ed., *Equal Shares: Making Market Socialism Work* (London/New York: Verso, 1996), pp. 93–109.

4 On the significance and the limits of Marx' economic theory, see Heimann, *Geschichte der volkswirtschaftlichen Lehrmeinungen*, ch. VI.

5 On this discussion, see Wright, ed., *Equal Shares*.

6 A major exception in Marx' work, in which he usually speaks of "capitalism" as an "eternal structure" (Max Weber) can be found in his "Inaugural Address of the International Workers' Association", in which he speaks of a struggle between the "political economy of the middle class" and that of the "working class" over the best mode of production. In this context he calls the "co-operative movement" and "co-operative factories" "great social experiments", as if he wished to concede that the task of "social production controlled by social foresight" is a matter of experimentally exploring the possibilities of the (capitalist) market: Karl Marx, "Inaugural Address of the Working Men's International Association", in *Marx and Engels: Collected Works, Vol. 20* (Moscow: Progress Publishers, 1982), pp. 5–13. For a critique of Marx' understanding of capitalism as a system that operates according to timeless laws, see Honneth, "Die Moral im 'Kapital': Versuch einer Korrektur der Marxschen Ökonomiekritik".

7 On the first tendency, see Thomas Piketty, *Capital in the Twenty-First Century* (Cambridge, MA: Belknap, 2014); on the second tendency, see Wolfgang Streeck, *Buying Time: The Delayed Crisis of Democratic Capitalism* (London: Verso, 2014), esp. ch. III.

8 Adam Smith, *The Wealth of Nations* (London: Penguin Classics, 1999); see Lisa Herzog, *Inventing the Market: Smith, Hegel, and Political Thought* (Oxford: Oxford University Press, 2013).

9 On the distinctions between these three models, see Erik Olin Wright, *Envisioning Real Utopias* (London: Verso, 2010), ch. 7.

10 Herzog, *Inventing the Market*; Samuel Fleischacker, *On Adam Smith's 'Wealth of Nations': A Philosophical Companion* (Princeton, NJ: Princeton University Press, 2004), part II.

11 See Dewey, *Liberalism and Social Action*, pp. 41–65.

12 Ibid.; see also John Dewey, "The Inclusive Philosophic Idea", in *Later Works, Vol. 3*, pp. 41–54. See also John Dewey, *Experience and Nature, The Later Works of John Dewey, Vol. 1* (Carbondale, IL: Southern Illinois University Press, 1988), ch. 5.

13 Dewey, "The Inclusive Philosophic Idea", p. 43.

14 Dewey, *Lectures in China, 1919–1920*, pp. 64–71. I owe this reference to the particularity of Dewey's approach to Arvi Särkelä; see his essay "Ein Drama in drei Akten: Der Kampf um öffentliche Anerkennung nach Dewey und Hegel", *Deutsche Zeitschrift für Philosophie*, vol. 61 (2013), pp. 681–96.

15 John Dewey clearly saw the resemblance of his own conception of a force within the "social" that brushes aside limitations on communication to Hegel's idea of historical progress. See John Dewey, "Lecture on Hegel", in J.R. Shock & J.A. Good, *John Dewey's Philosophy of Spirit* (New York: Fordham University Press, 2010). For an interpretation of Hegel's philosophy of history in the sense mentioned here, see the impressive interpretation

provided by Rahel Jaeggi, *Kritik von Lebensformen* (Berlin: Suhrkamp, 2013), pp. 423ff.

16 On the logic of such a historical experimentalism, see ibid., ch. 10.1.

17 In my view this is what separates socialism from the theoretical self-understanding of John Rawls' conception of justice, which he has continually refined over the years with astounding clarity and caution. Rawls believes that the task of a political conception of justice is to draw the attention of the members of democratic societies to the principles of fairness to which they must consent given the ideals they already accept, thus reconciling these ideals with already existing institutions (John Rawls, *Justice as Fairness: A Restatement* (Cambridge, MA: Belknap Press, 2001)). By contrast, socialism, believing itself to be the expression of a historical tendency, seeks to point out those unfulfilled promises in the existing social order, the fulfillment of which requires a transformation of institutional structures. The distinction between the two theories, therefore, does not merely concern their ethical point of reference – individual autonomy in Rawls' case, social freedom in socialism's case – but also their practical and political perspective. Rawls aims at ethical reconciliation, while socialism must strive for permanent transgression.

18 Pierre-Joseph Proudhon, *Solution of the Social Problem*, cited in Cole, *Socialist Thought*, p. 217.

19 See the famous formulation by Dewey with reference to the idea of democracy: "Regarded as an idea, democracy is not an alternative to other principles of associated life. It is the idea of community

life itself. It is an ideal in the only intelligible sense of an ideal: namely, the tendency and movement of some thing which exists carried to its final limit, viewed as completed, perfected" (John Dewey, "The Public and its Problems" in *John Dewey: The Later Works, 1925–1953, Vol.* 2 (Carbondale, IL: Southern Illinois University Press, 1984), p. 328).

20 The premise for this task is the same that guided Marx, and it consists in viewing the capitalist economy as being already mediated or co-produced by the theoretical terminology of dominant economic theory, meaning that we can only call reality into question by criticizing the theory. See especially Michael Theunissen, "Möglichkeiten des Philosophierens heute", in *Negative Theologie der Zeit* (Frankfurt/Main: Suhrkamp, 1991), pp. 13–36, esp. pp. 21ff. Unlike Marx, I believe that the object of such a critique of the dominant economic theory should not be the concept of the "market" itself, rather its internal melding with capitalist particularities.

21 Karl Polanyi, *The Great Transformation: The Political and Economic Origins of Our Time* (Boston, MA: Beacon Press, 2001); Amitai Etzioni, *The Moral Dimensions: Towards a New Economy* (New York: The Free Press, 1988); Albert O. Hirschman, *Entwicklung, Markt, Moral: Abweichende Bemerkungen* (Munich/Vienna: Hanser, 1989). On the significance of Etzioni and Hirschman in this context, see Axel Honneth, *Vivisektionen eines Zeitalters: Porträts zur Ideengeschichte des 20. Jahrhunderts* (Berlin: Suhrkamp, 2014), chs 7 and 8.

22 Friedrich Kambartel, *Philosophie und politische*

Ökonomie (Göttingen: Wallstein, 1998), esp. pp. 11–40.

23 Ibid., p. 25.

24 See John Roemer, "Ideology, Social Ethos, and the Financial Crisis", *Journal of Ethics*, vol. 16, no. 3 (2012), pp. 273–303.

25 On the problematic issue of the right to inheritance, see Jens Beckert, *Unverdientes Vermögen: Zur Soziologie des Erbrechts* (Frankfurt/Main: Campus, 2004); Beckert, "Erbschaft und Leistungsprinzip", in *Erben in der Leistungsgesellschaft* (Frankfurt/Main: Campus, 2013), pp. 41–64; on the idea of common ownership among producers, see Kambartel, *Philosophie und politische Ökonomie*, pp. 32ff.

26 With the term "end in view" Dewey sought to express the fact that final aims should never be understood as fixed goals, but rather as variables that must be constantly adapted to new experiences: The "end in view" is a "constant and cumulative reenactment at each stage of forward movement. It is no longer a terminal point, external to the conditions that have led up to it; it is the continual developing meaning of present tendencies – the very thing as directed we call 'means'. The process is art and its product, no matter at what stage it be taken, is a work of art." If socialism had adopted this transformed understanding of ends and means at a much earlier stage, it would have been spared many of the evils deriving from the use of the term "final aim" (Dewey, *Experience and Nature*, p. 280).

27 For a clear overview of the fronts in this debate, see Karl Polanyi, "Die funktionelle Theorie der

Gesellschaft und das Problem der sozialistischen Rechnungslegung (Eine Erwiderung an Professor Mises und Dr. Felix Weil)", in: *Ökonomie und Gesellschaft* (Frankfurt/Main: Campus, 1979, pp. 81–90). (I owe this reference to Christoph Deutschmann.)

28 For the first alternative, see Michael Nance, "Honneth's Democratic *Sittlichkeit* and Market Socialism" (unpublished manuscript) (2014); John Roemer, *A Future for Socialism* (Cambridge, MA: Harvard University Press, 1994); for the other alternative, see Diane Elson, "Markt-Sozialismus oder Sozialisierung des Marktes", *Prokla*, vol. 20, no. 78 (1990), pp. 60–106. The distinction between these two types of post-capitalist economic systems is similar to the distinction John Rawls makes between "property-owning democracy" and "liberal socialism" (Rawls, *Justice as Fairness*, pp. 215–18). For an overview, see Jon Elster and Karl Ove Moene, eds, *Alternatives to Capitalism* (Cambridge: Cambridge University Press, 1989).

29 On this principle, see the valuable study by Michael Festl, *Gerechtigkeit als historischer Experimentalismus: Gerechtigkeitstheorie nach der pragmatischen Wende der Erkenntnistheorie* (Konstanz: Konstanz University Press, 2015), pp. 407–9. On the extremely difficult question posed to me by Andrea Esser about how socialist experiments in the past could be falsified today given historically changed conditions, the following principle is a good start: Experiments resulting in the violation of established practices for will-formation in line with the rule of law must be viewed as having failed.

30 On the task of putting together such an "encyclopedia of past cases" in connection with historical experimentalism, see again the study by Michael Festl, *Gerechtigkeit als historischer Experimentalismus*, pp. 402–23.

31 The poor state that the project of socialism finds itself in today is made apparent by the fact that hardly any of these documents can currently be found in an edited form. The ups and downs of the movement can be easily traced by looking at the offerings in bookstores: Whereas 40 or 50 years ago the publisher Rowohlt offered a solid collection of books on "socialism and anarchism" which contained important testaments from the past, it has long since disappeared from the list of deliverable publications.

32 Wright, *Envisioning Real Utopias*, esp. ch. 7.

33 See Festl, *Gerechtigkeit als historischer Experimentalismus*, pp. 387ff.

34 On the situation of the service proletariat today, see the following two impressive studies: Friederike Bahl, *Lebensmodelle in der Dienstleistungsgesellschaft* (Hamburg: HIS, 2014); Philipp Staab, *Macht und Herrschaft in der Servicewelt* (Hamburg: HIS, 2014).

35 On the status of this Kantian concept in the philosophy of history, see Axel Honneth, "The Irreducibility of Progress: Kant's Account of the Relationship Between Morality and History", in *Pathologies of Reason: On the Legacy of Critical Theory* (New York: Columbia University Press, 2009).

IV. Paths of Renewal (2): The Idea of a Democratic Form of Life

1 Conversely, this means that wherever the term "democratic socialism" was not used, there remained a conceptually opaque opposition between "democracy" and "socialism/communism". An example of this can be found in Arthur Rosenberg, *Democracy and Socialism: A Contribution to the Political History of the Past 150 Years* (London: Bell, 1939).

2 See the illuminating overview by Niklas Luhmann, *Die Gesellschaft der Gesellschaft* (Frankfurt/Main: Suhrkamp, 1997), ch. 4.VII, pp. 707–43. A good account of the problem can also be found in Hartmann Tyrell, "Anfragen an die Theorie der gesellschaftlichen Differenzierung", *Zeitschrift für Soziologie*, vol. 7, no. 2 (1978), pp. 175–93.

3 On all the differentiations made by early liberals, see Stephen Holmes, "Differenzierung und Arbeitsteilung im Denken des Liberalismus", in N. Luhmann, ed., *Soziale Differenzierung* (Opladen: Westdeutscher Verlag, 1985), pp. 9–41.

4 G.W.F. Hegel, *Elements of the Philosophy of Right* (Cambridge: Cambridge University Press, 1991).

5 Karl Marx, *Critique of Hegel's 'Philosophy of Right'*, J. O'Malley, ed. (Cambridge: Cambridge University Press, 1970).

6 On this perspective, in opposition to Niklas Luhmann's approach, see Uwe Schimank & Ute Volkmann, "Ökonomisierung der Gesellschaft", in A. Maurer, ed., *Handbuch der Wirtschaftssoziologie* (Wiesbaden: Springer Verlag, 2008), pp. 382–93.

7 Jürgen Habermas, *Between Facts and Norms* (Cambridge, MA: MIT Press, 1996), ch. 3.

8 Ibid., ch. 4.

9 On this problem, see Wolfgang Mager, "Republik", in *Geschichtliche Grundbegriffe: Historisches Lexikon zur politisch-sozialen Sprache in Deutschland*, Vol. 5, pp. 549–651, here: pp. 639–48. In this subchapter on the discussion in the German workers' movement over socialists' relation to republicanism, it is also mentioned that both Marx ("Critique of the Gotha Program", in *Karl Marx: Selected Writings*, Lawrence H. Simon, ed. (Indianapolis, IN: Hackett, 1994), pp. 315–32) and Engels (Friedrich Engels, "A Critique of the Draft Social-Democratic Program of 1891", in *Marx/Engels Selected Works, Vol. 3* (Moscow: Progress Publishers) occasionally agreed for tactical reasons to the aims of democratic republicanism. The extremely problematic relationship between the socialists and radical republicanism is also dealt with in Robert Wuthnow's *Communities of Discourse*, pp. 367ff.

10 On Julius Fröbel, see Jürgen Habermas, "Popular Sovereignty as Procedure", in *Between Facts and Norms*, pp. 463–90; on Léon Gambetta, see Daniel Mollenhauer, *Auf der Suche nach der "wahren Republik": Die französischen "radicaux" in der frühen Dritten Republik (1870–1890)*, esp. chs 3, 4 and 5.

11 See his posthumously published polemic: Pierre-Joseph Proudhon, *La Pornocratie, ou Les femmes dans les temps modernes* (Paris: A. Lacroix, 1875).

12 On the role of Barthélemy-Prosper Enfantin in connection with the use of Saint-Simonism for the aims of women's liberation, see Salomon-Delatour's

"Introduction", in *Die Lehre Saint-Simons*, pp. 9–31, esp. pp. 20ff.

13 Friedrich Engels, *The Origin of the Family, Private Property and the State* (London: Penguin Classics, 2010). For a critique on Engels' text, especially its "economic monism", see Simone de Beauvoir, *The Second Sex* (New York: Vintage Books, 1989), p. 52.

14 See Honneth, *Freedom's Right*, ch. C.III.1.

15 On the unfortunate relationship between the workers' movement and the women's movement in the second half of the nineteenth century, see Ute Gerhard, *Frauenbewegung und Feminismus: Eine Geschichte seit 1789* (Munich: Beck, 2009), pp. 57–9. See also Mechthild Merfeld, *Die Emanzipation der Frau in der sozialistischen Theorie und Praxis* (Reinbek bei Hamburg: Rowohlt, 1972), part 2.

16 See the illuminating reconstruction by Antje Schrupp, "Feministischer Sozialismus? Gleichheit und Differenz in der Geschichte des Sozialismus", available at: https://www.antjeschrupp.de/feministis cher-sozialismus/.

17 August Bebel comes closest to the notion that women's liberation from the constraints of traditional understandings of marriage and the family requires an independent semantics of freedom with his classic work *Woman and Socialism* (New York: Socialist Literature Co., 1910). However, even Bebel has the tendency to regard "bourgeois marriage" as a "result of bourgeois property relations" and thus to restrict himself to the perspective of collectivizing the conditions of production without treating familial relations of socialization themselves (see ch. 28).

18 For a useful clarification of the concept, which is also applicable to a theory of society, see Kristina Schulz, *Der lange Arm der Provokation: Die Frauenbewegung in der Bundesrepublik und in Frankreich 1968–1976* (Frankfurt/Main: Campus, 2002), ch. V.2.

19 On the history of this calamitous distinction, see Wolfgang Fritz Haug & Isabel Monal, "Grundwiderspruch, Haupt-/Nebenwiderspruch", in W.F. Haug, ed., *Historisch-kritisches Wörterbuch des Marxismus*, Vol. 5 (Hamburg: Argument, 2001), pp. 1040–50.

20 We can see how strong are the effects of this fatal legacy of socialism – the inability to take account of functional differentiation – even today by considering the socio-theoretical naivety with which Gerald Cohen, even in 2009, sketches a vision of a future social society without even speaking of the division between different spheres with their own logics of action. Instead, he presents a model of a future society in the form of a camp in which there are no stable divisions between different social tasks organized according to specific rules (Gerald A. Cohen, *Why Not Socialism?* Princeton, NJ: Princeton University Press, 2009). How fitting is the comment by Emile Durkheim, a committed proponent of the necessity of functional differentiations that social life could never consist in "military life". Emile Durkheim, *Moral Education: A Study in the Theory and Application of the Sociology of Education* (New York: Free Press, 1961), p. 160.

21 See Axel Honneth, "Drei, nicht zwei Begriffe der Freiheit: Ein Vorschlag zur Erweiterung

unseres moralischen Selbstverständnisses", in O. Mitscherlich-Schönherr & M. Schlossberger, eds, *Die Unergründlichkeit der menschlichen Natur* (Berlin: Akademie, 2015).

22 As a continuation of the justification I gave above for the socialist task of subjecting dominant economic theories to critique (see note 20 in chapter III), socialism must always also offer a critique of those dominant theories that also contribute to producing social reality in the spheres of personal relationships and political will-formation, e.g. standard liberal models of the family or the dominant theory of democracy, which is firmly anchored in the concept of negative freedom. If we accept the moral fact of functional differentiation in the sense presented here in a strongly Hegelian manner, then it is not enough to present a critique of political economy. Instead, we must also offer a critique of hegemonial branches of knowledge that deal with the other constitutive subsystems and whose concepts have always contributed to creating the reality within these subsystems.

23 This tripartite division of the constitutive spheres does not only, by the way, coincide with Hegel and Durkheim (on Durkheim, see *Physik der Sitten und der Moral: Vorlesungen zur Soziologie der Moral* (Frankfurt/Main: Suhrkamp, 1999)), but also with the differentiations made by John Rawls with reference to the "basic structure" of society, which he regards to be the main object of a theory of justice. See Rawls, *Justice as Fairness*, p. 10.

24 The best study on Hegel's use of the conception of the organism in his philosophy of right can be

found in Michael Wolff, "Hegels staatstheoretischer Organismus: Zum Begriff und zur Methode der Hegelschen 'Staatswissenschaft'", *Hegel-Studien*, vol. 19 (1985), pp. 147–77. Here we also find indications of how Marx picks up on this methodological element in Hegel's doctrine of the state in order to make it useful for his own theory: Ibid., pp. 149f. On the use of the conception of an organism in German Idealism, see Ernst-Wolfgang Böckenförde, "Organ, Organismus, Organisation, politischer Körper", in *Geschichtliche Grundbegriffe: Historisches Lexikon zur politisch-sozialen Sprache in Deutschland*, Vol. 4, pp. 519–622, here: pp. 579–86.

25 With reference to Durkheim, who makes systematic use of the analogy of an organism, see Hartmann Tyrell, "Emile Durkheim – Das Dilemma der organischen Solidariät", in N. Luhmann, ed., *Soziale Differenzierung*, pp. 181–250.

26 This famous formulation stems from the preface to Marx's *A Contribution to the Critique of Political Economy*: "At a certain stage of development, the material productive forces of society come into conflict with the existing relations of production or – this merely expresses the same thing in legal terms – with the property relations within the framework of which they have operated hitherto. From forms of development of the productive forces these relations turn into their fetters. Then begins an era of social revolution" (Karl Marx, "Preface to *A Contribution to the Critique of Political Economy*" in *Karl Marx: Selected Writings*, pp. 209–13, here: p. 211).

27 On the conception of an organism in the work of

Marx, see Lars Hennings, *Marx, Engels und die Teilung der Arbeit: Ein einführendes Lesebuch in Gesellschaftstheorie und Geschichte* (Berlin: GRIN Verlag, 2012), pp. 204f.

28 The idea of understanding democracy not only as a political form of government, but as an entire way of life, stems from John Dewey (see John Dewey, *Democracy and Education*, in *The Middle Works [1899–1924]*, Vol. 9 (Carbondale, IL: University of Southern Illinois Press, 1985), here: pp. 92–4; "The Public and Its Problems", p. 329). Sidney Hook, a student of Dewey, would later pick up this notion and further refine it in "Democracy as a Way of Life", *Southern Review*, vol. 4 (1938), pp. 46–57; see also Roberto Frega, *Le pragmatisme comme philosophie sociale et politique* (Lormont: Le Bord de l'eau, 2015), pp. 113–33. I agree with the tradition of pragmatism here, but expand it by adding the systematic thought of functional differentiation in order to determine the spheres of action whose democratic and associative structure allow them to make up an entire way of life.

29 Here I pick up on the liberal thought of Michael Walzer in order to make it fruitful for the idea of socialism: Michael Walzer, "Liberalism and the Art of Separation", *Political Theory*, vol. 12, no. 3 (1984), pp. 315–30.

30 For a critique of this premise of the dominant theory of differentiation, see Uwe Schimank, "Der mangelnde Akteursbezug systemtheoretischer Erklärungen gesellschaftlicher Differenzierung", *Zeitschrift für Soziologie*, vol. 14 (1985), pp. 421–34.

31 On the history of this discussion, which reaches far back into the past, see the collection by G. Haupt, M. Lowy & C. Weill, *Les Marxistes et la question nationale 1848–1914: Études et textes* (Paris: Maspero, 1949).

32 See Dewey, *The Public and Its Problems*.

33 Durkheim, *Physik der Sitten und der Moral*, pp. 115ff.

34 Jürger Habermas, *The Structural Transformation of the Public Sphere: An Inquiry into a Category of Bourgeois Society* (Cambridge: Polity, 1989). There remain a number of significant differences between Dewey's "functionalist" conception and Habermas' "institutionalist" conception (and that of Hannah Arendt). These differences become less pronounced, however, the more Habermas comes to grasp the public sphere merely as a medium of civil society (Habermas, *Between Facts and Norms*, ch. 8).

35 See above, pp. 61ff.

36 On the epistemic role of the movements that are formed and articulated in the democratic public sphere, see Elizabeth Anderson, "The Epistemology of Democracy", *Episteme. A Journal of Social Epistemology*, vol. 3, no. 1 (2006), pp. 8–22.

37 On this perspective, see Hans Joas, *The Creativity of Action* (Cambridge: Polity, 1996), ch. 4.3.

38 See above, pp. 73f.

39 On the attendant difficulties of such a project, see Kate Nash, ed., *Transnationalizing the Public Sphere* (Cambridge, MA: MIT Press, 2014).

40 See Forschungsgruppe Weltgesellschaft, "Weltgesellschaft: Identifizierung eines 'Phantoms'", *Politische Vierteljahreszeitschrift*, vol. 37, no.

1 (1996), pp. 5–26; Lothar Brock & Mathias Albert, "Entgrenzung der Staatenwelt: Zur Analyse weltgesellschaftlicher Entwicklungstendenzen", *Zeitschrift für Internationale Beziehungen*, vol. 2, no. 2 (1995), pp. 259–85.

41 Tyrell, "Anfragen an die Theorie der gesellschaftlichen Differenzierung", p. 187.

42 Ulrich Beck & Edgar Grande, "Jenseits des methodologischen Nationalismus: Außereuropäische und europäische Variationen der Zweiten Moderne", *Soziale Welt*, no. 61 (2010), pp. 187–216.

43 Piketty, *Capital in the Twenty-First Century*, ch. 14.

44 See John Rawls, "Justice as Fairness: Political not Metaphysical", *Philosophy and Public Affairs*, vol. 14 (1985), pp. 223–51.

45 Socialism, however, is a "global theory", to use John Rawls' terminology, which offers good reasons for hoping to become, unlike other "global theories", a theoretical platform for an "overlapping consensus" under conditions of "rational pluralism".

Index

Index

Index

feminism 84, 85–7
fetishistic conception of social
    relations 4
feudal-bourgeois property
    order 37, 43
Feuerbach, Ludwig 17
Fourier, Charles 8, 11, 34
Fourierists 7, 8, 9
Frankfurt School 40
fraternity 13, 15, 16, 17,
    18, 21, 29, 54, 77, 78,
    115
    freedom and 11, 12, 13, 14,
        15, 78
    French Revolution principle
        6, 27
free market philosophy 47
freedom
    capitalistic 15, 18, 32
    and fraternity 11, 12, 13,
        14, 15, 78
    as free cooperation 13
    French Revolution principle
        6
    Hegelian theory of 37
    individualistic
        understanding of 11, 14,
        15, 20–1, 54, 77
    institutionalized 83
    intersubjective relationships
        and 13, 14, 27
    legal understanding of 11,
        32
    liberal rights to 12, 21, 35,
        36, 37
    Marxist conception of
        18–19, 20
    negative understanding of
        21

new, positive concept of 13,
    21–2
"objective" 23
private and egotistic 12, 32,
    34, 36
republican understanding of
    22
and solidarity, reconciling
    14, 15, 18, 36, 66, 78
    see also social freedom
French Revolution 6, 9, 10,
    14, 27, 32, 76, 83
    contradictions of 11, 12,
        25, 51
    founding documents 82
    post-revolutionary France
        8–9, 42–3
    principles of 8, 11, 27, 64
Fröbel, Julius 83
functional differentiation of
    society 77, 78, 79–80, 81,
    83, 85, 86, 87–8, 95, 97,
    100, 132, 133

Gambetta, Léon 83
gay marriage 100
gender equality 87
global society 100
global tax 102
goal-realization, collective 19
Greenpeace 102
Grotius, Hugo 6

Habermas, Jürgen 52, 96, 136
Hegel, G.W.F. 16, 22, 23, 37,
    44, 60, 62–3, 64, 73, 90–1
    Phenomenology of Spirit 17
    Philosophy of Right 35, 79,
        80

Index

Index

Index

Index